DEALING
WITH
DELINQUENCY

An Investigation of
Juvenile Justice

Jay S. Albanese, Ph.D.

UNIVERSITY
PRESS OF
AMERICA

LANHAM • NEW YORK • LONDON

University Press of America,™ Inc.

4720 Boston Way
Lanham, MD 20706

3 Henrietta Street
London WC2E 8LU England

Library of Congress Cataloging in Publication Data

Albanese, Jay S.
  Dealing with delinquency.

  Includes bibliographies and index.
  1. Juvenile justice, Administration of—United States.
2. Juvenile delinquency—United States. I. Title.
HV9104.A73   1984   364.3'6'0973   84-25657
ISBN 0-8191-4448-7 (alk. paper)
ISBN 0-8191-4449-5 (pbk. : alk. paper)

To

all current and former hidden delinquents,

that they may better understand

the prospects for those who were caught

JAY S. ALBANESE received the B.A. degree from Niagara University and M.A. and Ph.D. from the School of Criminal Justice at Rutgers University. He is author of the books IS PROBATION WORKING? [1981], ORGANIZATIONAL OFFENDERS [1982], MYTHS & REALITIES OF CRIME AND JUSTICE [1983], and JUSTICE, PRIVACY, AND CRIME CONTROL [1984]. Dr. Albanese is currently a professor of Criminology and Criminal Justice at Niagara University.

ACKNOWLEDGEMENTS

My intellectual debts are many. Although they are not recognized explicitly in this book, the autobiographical accounts of Claude Brown, Piri Thomas, John Allen, and Waln Brown have done much to make the experiences of delinquents and the problems of the juvenile justice system more urgent to me, as well as to my students. The contribution of students to this manuscript can not be underestimated either. It is undoubtedly true that the best way to understand every aspect of a problem is to teach another about it.

Perhaps the most significant fact reported in this book is that nearly everyone engages in delinquent behavior at one time or another during their youth. Although common sense (which apparently is not so common) would indicate that this is so, there is an overwhelming tendency to react intensely against those caught by police for acts of delinquency. "Lock him up to teach him a lesson!" "Send them to prison until they rot!" are common anthems in contemporary society. It appears we quickly forget our activities as juveniles and fail to consider how our lives might have been changed if we had been caught and adjudicated for those acts of shoplifting, vandalism, fighting, or truancy. We fail to consider how our circle of friends might have changed from the kids on the block to the kids in the institution, from our parents care to the care of state employees, from a college education to something less promising. It is for these reasons that an understanding of delinquency is really an understanding of ourselves. Until we realize there is no "us" v. "them", that there is only "us", there is little hope for justice for juvenile delinquents.

The remainder of this book provides the details for understanding delinquency and juvenile justice. I have made a conscious effort to be concise without oversimplfying issues. The references following each chapter provide further explanation of the points raised in each section. I hope you find the presentation interesting; a conversation about human behavior usually is.

Once again, my Kaypro microcomputer has served faithfully as a secretary and editor. It has allowed me to change my mind on numerous occasions with only minimal discomfort. To this day, I do not understand how I ever wrote my dissertation without it. Also, my cat, Snagglepuss, deserves some credit for constantly demanding to be let in and out of the house. She caused me to reconsider many issues on my way up and down the stairs.

CONTENTS

1. WHAT IS DELINQUENCY?

THE AGE FACTOR

In the eyes of the law, the only difference between a juvenile delinquent and an adult criminal is age. If a criminal act is committed by a person under the age of majority in his or her state, the act is considered delinquency. If the illegal act is committed by someone who has reached the age of majority, that person has committed a crime. Therefore, the only difference between a criminal act and an act of juvenile delinquency is the age of the offender.

Let's say you miss the bus downtown on your way to a party. Because it is too far to walk and you do not wish to wait for the next bus, you steal a car and proceed to drive downtown. If you are caught, you would be subject to the penalties for motor vehicle theft. But how would you know if your trial would be held in criminal (adult) court or in juvenile court? As it turns out, your age at the time you committed the act would determine which court has jurisdiction. Depending upon the state, a person becomes an adult in the eyes of the law at anywhere from age 16 to age 21. In most states, however, a person becomes an adult at age 18. In addition, if you are under a certain age (8 years old in many states) you cannot be held legally responsible for an illegal act. This is because small children are not seen as being old enough to fully understand the consequences of their actions. Therefore, they cannot be adjudicated in criminal or juvenile court.

This book is directed, therefore, at the unlawful acts of persons between the ages of approximately 8 to 18. The nature and extent of illegal acts committed by this age group, the causes and prevention of their misbehavior, and how the juvenile justice system is designed to adjudicate persons charged with these acts will be explained. It is hoped that this presentation will eliminate some of the myths that pervade discussions of juvenile delinquency and will help to establish the basis for improvements in the juvenile justice system and in society in general to more effectively prevent serious delinquency in the future.

STATUS OFFENDERS

Besides delinquency, there are acts for which juveniles can be forced to appear in juvenile court. These acts are called status offenses and do not involve violations of the criminal law. In fact, these acts are merely undesirable behaviors that are unlawful only for juveniles. Examples of status offenses include: habitual truancy from school, curfew violations, repeated runaways, and ungovernability or incorrigibility.

The range of behaviors considered status offenses is not uniform nationwide and varies greatly among the states. Some states include the use of alcohol, tobacco, marijuana, profanity, or having delinquent associates, as status offenses. Also, states refer to status offenders with slightly different legal terminology. In New York State, for example, they are called P.I.N.S. (Persons in Need of Supervision), in New Jersey, J.I.N.S. (Juveniles in Need of Supervision), and in Washington, D.C., CH.I.N.S. (Children in Need of Supervision).

Therefore, juveniles can be taken into custody, adjudicated, and incarcerated for the commission of status offenses, as well as for delinquency. As a result, the juvenile justice system deals with two distinct types of persons: delinquents and status offenders.

JUVENILE JUSTICE v. CRIMINAL JUSTICE

Because of their age, juveniles are treated separately from adults in the justice process. Police often have officers who deal exclusively with juveniles. Every state has a separate juvenile court system which deals exclusively with juveniles. In addition, every state has separate facilities for the incarceration of juvenile offenders.

The legal status of juveniles in this justice process is also unique, and it differs significantly from the adult system. For example, the case involving motor vehicle theft, described earlier, would be handled quite differently depending on the age of the offender. As an adult, the official charge would be motor vehicle theft, but in the case of a juvenile the charge would simply be delinquency. In a criminal case, the defendant's name, the court proceedings, and trial transcripts would all be a matter of public record. In juvenile court, however, all of this information would be confidential and is withheld from the public. Finally, upon a finding of guilt the adult would be convicted of motor vehicle theft, whereas the juvenile would be adjudicated a delinquent. The reason for this disparate treatment of juveniles and adults in the justice process is largely a function of history.

At the turn of the century, it was argued that equal treatment of juveniles and adults in the eyes of the law violated the principles of American ideology. According to this view, minors who broke the law were actually victims of improper parental care and treatment at home. When juveniles broke the law, it was a sign that the parents could not or would not adequately take care of the child, and it was up to the state to step in and act in the best interests of this child (to prevent future misbehavior). This view is called parens patriae (state to act as parent).

The philosophy of parens patriae meant that the state should not punish children for their criminal behavior but should try to help them to control and prevent future criminality. As a result, it made no sense to convict children of such crimes as motor vehicle theft, or burglary, or robbery because such a label would stigmatize them as criminals. Instead, the label of delinquency was used to indicate that the child needed the care and treatment of the state. It was upon this notion of parens patriae that the first juvenile court was established in the United States in 1899.

In recent years, however, considerable controversy has arisen over the legal treatment of juveniles. The effectiveness of the state in acting as a surrogate parent has been questioned, the adequacy of the legal protections of juveniles in court, and whether the parens patriae philosophy should be abandoned (in favor of the treatment of juveniles as adults) has been considered. Each of these issues will be addressed in subsequent chapters of this book.

Similar controversy has arisen in the handling of status offenders in the juvenile justice process. Serious allegations regarding the incarceration of status offenders for non-serious behavior, vagueness in the definitions of some status offenses, whether status offenders and delinquents should be adjudicated separately, whether juvenile justice processing makes status offenders better or worse, and whether status offenses should be abolished altogether, have all drawn attention in recent years.

These issues of adjudication will be addressed in subsequent chapters. First, it is important to understand the true extent of delinquency and whether or not it is becoming an increasing threat in American life.

2. ARE JUVENILES BECOMING MORE DELINQUENT?

OFFICIAL DELINQUENCY

Establishing the true extent of delinquency helps citizens to assess their actual risk of being victimized. It also helps public officials determine the relative urgency that should be attached to delinquency prevention efforts. Unfortunately, the precise level and types of delinquent acts are more difficult to establish than is commonly believed.

Many people rely on the FBI's annual Uniform Crime Reports (UCR) which records all crimes known to the police. This compilation is of little use, however, because: (1) It is impossible to know whether the perpetrators of these crimes are juveniles or adults, and (2) It has been found through victimization surveys (interviews with a representative sample of U.S. citizens) that less than 50 percent of all serious crime is actually reported to the police. As a result, alternate measures of the extent of delinquency must be relied upon.

The most commonly used indicator of delinquency has been the proportion of crime suspects arrested that are juveniles. Juvenile arrests certainly provide information about the age of suspects and, assuming that the proportion of juvenile offenders who are arrested does not fluctuate widely from year-to-year, it is possible to see if juveniles are becoming more or less responsible for criminal behavior in the United States. Table 1 summarizes the proportion of arrests during the last nine years that have involved juveniles.

As Table 1 indicates, there were 10.1 million arrests made in the United States in 1982. Of these, 1.8 million were juveniles--a total of 17.9 percent. This means that of the more than 10 million arrests made by police during 1982, only about 18 percent of them were arrests of juveniles. The 28 crimes listed in Table 1 are all those offenses which are considered in the FBI's annual compilation of arrest data. The first eight offenses, collectively, are called the Crime Index and are often used as a barometer of serious crime in the United States. The crimes of criminal homicide, forcible rape, robbery, and aggravated assault are considered violent crime (i.e., crimes against persons), while the crimes of burglary, larceny, motor vehicle theft, and arson are considered property crimes (i.e., property is the victim). The FBI's definitions of these crimes are listed below.

Criminal Homicide. Murder and non-negligent manslaughter: all willful and felonious homicides as distinguished from deaths caused by negligence, and excludes attempts to kill, assaults to kill, suicides, accidental deaths, or justifiable homicides. Justifiable homicides are limited to: [1] the killing of a felon by a law enforcement officer in the line of duty, and [2] the killing of a person in the act of committing a felony by a private citizen.

Forcible Rape. The carnal knowledge of a female forcibly and against her will in the categories of rape by force and attempts or assaults to rape. Excludes statutory offenses [no force and victim under age of consent].

Robbery. Stealing or taking anything of value from the care, custody, or control of a person by force or by violence or by putting in fear, such as strong-arm robbery, armed robbery, attempts or assaults to rob.

Aggravated Assault. Assault with intent to kill or for the purpose of inflicting severe bodily injury by shooting, cutting, stabbing, maiming, poisoning, scalding, or by the use of acids, explosives, or other means. Excludes simple assaults.

Burglary. House-breaking or any breaking or unlawful entry with intent to commit a felony or theft. Includes attempted forcible entry.

Larceny. The unlawful taking, carrying, leading, or riding away of property from the possession or constructive possession of another. Thefts of bicycles, automobile accessories, shoplifting, pocket-picking, or any stealing of property or article which is not taken by force and violence or fraud. Excludes embezzlement, "con" games, forgery, worthless checks, etc.

Motor Vehicle Theft. Unlawful taking or attempted theft of a motor vehicle. A motor vehicle is self-propelled and travels on the surface rather than on the rails. Specifically excluded from this category are motorboats, construction equipment, airplanes, and farming equipment.

Table 1. Arrests of Persons Under 18 Years of Age
(Percentage of total arrests, 1975-1982)

Offenses	1975	1977	1979	1981	1982
Criminal Homicide	9.5	9.7	9.3	9.1	8.5
Forcible Rape	17.6	16.5	15.9	14.8	14.7
Robbery	34.3	32.0	31.5	28.6	26.4
Aggravated Assault	17.6	16.3	15.5	14.0	13.2
Burglary	52.6	51.5	48.6	42.6	39.6
Larceny	45.1	42.9	40.4	34.8	32.4
Motor Vehicle Theft	54.5	53.0	49.2	40.5	36.0
Arson	53.0	49.8	49.0	42.4	37.2
Total Violent Crimes	23.1	21.0	20.1	18.5	17.2
Total Property Crime	48.0	46.2	43.5	37.4	34.5
INDEX Total	43.1	41.2	38.8	33.5	30.9
Simple Assault	19.8	19.1	18.7	17.0	16.5
Forgery/Counterfeit	12.7	12.8	14.0	10.6	9.7
Fraud	3.2	10.3	3.4	5.2	7.0
Embezzlement	7.3	11.8	12.6	10.1	7.8
Stolen Property	32.6	32.9	33.1	27.0	24.7
Vandalism	65.4	60.3	54.2	47.4	44.3
Weapons Offenses	16.3	16.0	16.4	14.9	13.9
Prostitution	4.7	4.3	4.0	2.9	2.7
Other Sex Offenses	21.4	18.4	18.2	16.5	16.3
Drug Offenses	24.2	23.2	22.0	16.4	13.5
Gambling	3.6	4.2	4.1	3.3	3.5
Offenses Agst Family	11.8	5.9	4.8	4.6	3.5
DWI	1.9	2.2	2.4	2.0	1.8
Liquor Laws	39.6	37.3	36.0	30.6	29.4
Drunkenness	3.5	4.1	4.2	3.5	3.3
Disorderly Conduct	19.0	19.4	17.6	15.5	15.2
Vagrancy	9.0	12.7	14.3	11.3	11.3
Suspicion	26.5	26.5	27.1	20.5	15.8
Others (not traffic)	24.7	20.8	18.5	17.7	28.2
Curfew & Loitering	100	100	100	100	100
Runaways	100	100	100	100	100
Total % Juvenile	25.9	24.0	22.5	19.8	17.9
Total Arrests [in millions]	8M	9M	9.5M	9.7M	10.1M

Source: FBI Uniform Crime Reports.

Arson. Willful or malicious burning with or without intent to defraud. Includes attempts.

It can be seen in Table 1, for example, that 9.5 percent of all those arrested for criminal homicide in 1975 were juveniles. In 1982, the proportion of juveniles arrested for this crime had decreased slightly to 8.5 percent. Similarly, 54.5 percent of this arrested in 1975 for motor vehicle theft were juveniles. By 1982, this number had dropped to 36 percent.

Given this information, we can establish the crimes for which juveniles are most often arrested. First, it can be seen that every arrest for curfew and loitering violations, as well as runaways, was a juvenile. This is because these are status offenses which apply only to juveniles. The five crimes for which juveniles are most often arrested, other than status offenses, are presented in Table 2.

Table 2. Trends for Most Common Juvenile Arrests.
(Percentage of all arrests, 1975-1982)

Offenses	1975	1982	Percent change
Vandalism	65.4	44.3	-32%
Burglary	52.6	39.6	-25
Arson	53.0	37.2	-30
Motor Vehicle Theft	54.5	36.0	-40
Larceny	45.1	32.4	-28

The property crimes of vandalism, burglary, arson, motor vehicle theft, and larceny accounted for a higher proportion of juvenile arrests than any other crimes in 1975, a trend that continues to hold true in 1982. As Table 2 indicates, however, there has been a steady decrease in the proportion of juveniles arrested for these crimes during the last eight years.

As Table 1 shows, juveniles made up 29.5 percent of all arrests in 1973, and their proportion has steadily decreased to 17.9 percent in 1982. This holds true even though the total number of arrests (for juveniles and adults) has increased from 8 million in 1975 to 10.1 million in 1982.

So what does all of this mean? The only conclusion that can be drawn is that juveniles appear to be accounting for a shrinking proportion of the crime problem. That is, if arrests can be used as an indicator of criminal involvement, juveniles are committing proportionally fewer crimes than are adults. In 1975, juveniles accounted for better than half of all arrests for vandalism, burglary, motor vehicle theft, and arson in the United States. By 1982, however, juveniles did not comprise the majority of arrests in _any_ crime category counted by the FBI.

Unfortunately, arrests are not a good indicator of crime. In fact, arrests are a better measure of police activity than criminal activity. This is because changes in police practices, manpower allocations, and other factors, may affect the number of arrests that they make. As Table 3 illustrates, police arrests of juveniles to solve crimes (the clearance rate) take place in only about 21 percent of all cases. That is to say, of all arrests to solve crimes, only 21 percent of those arrested are juveniles. Further, this number has been decreasing steadily since 1975. Table 3 indicates that in 1975 police arrested juveniles to solve 30 percent of their cases and this percentage has dropped steadily to a clearance rate of 20.6 percent in 1982.

Table 3. Offenses Cleared By Arrest of Persons Under 18.
(Percentage of all clearances, 1975-1982)

Offense	1975	1977	1979	1981	1982
Criminal Homicide	4.9	5.4	5.0	4.6	4.0
Forcible Rape	9.4	10.1	9.4	9.4	10.0
Robbery	18.1	16.1	15.6	12.6	12.1
Aggravated Assault	11.0	10.5	10.6	9.0	8.8
Burglary	33.5	33.4	31.6	25.6	24.2
Larceny	35.2	32.8	31.0	24.7	24.2
Motor Vehicle Theft	32.0	30.9	27.7	20.7	18.8
Arson	NR	NR	NR	37.8	34.9
Crime INDEX Total	30.0	28.4	26.6	21.4	20.6

NR = Arson was not added to the Crime Index until 1980.
Source: FBI Uniform Crime Reports.

Arrests are not a good indicator of crime for other reasons as well. First, juveniles are over-represented in arrest statistics because they often commit less sophisticated crimes and are less mobile than adults. Therefore, they are less likely to escape detection. Second, many crimes are not reported to the police in the first place, making arrests even less representative of criminal activity. Due to a victim's fear of reprisal, embarrassment, lack of insurance, or belief that police can be of no assistance, victimization surveys have found that between two and four times more serious crime occurs than is reported to the police [Klaus, 1981]. Finally, changes in official statistics may reflect changes in police record-keeping practices. The 1967 President's Crime Commission, for example, told of how changes in reporting procedures in New York City and Chicago produced "paper" increases in crime, although the actual rates of crime had not changed significantly [1967:22-3]. For all of these reasons, it is imperative that an alternative is found to official statistics in determining the true extent of delinquency.

SELF-REPORT STUDIES

Self-reports provide an alternative way to measure the extent of delinquency. Self-report studies involve a sample of juveniles who anonymously report on a questionnaire, or to a confidential interviewer, the types and numbers of crimes they have committed in the past (whether or not they were caught). Self-reports were first attempted to see if there are differences between those juveniles who have been caught and those who have not. As sociologist, Albert Cohen, recognized 30 years ago,

> The defect of these [official] data, of course, is not that they represent too small a sample but that we cannot tell what sorts of delinquency and delinquencies may be overrepresented or underrepresented [1955:170].

Another purpose of self-report studies is, therefore, to separate those factors that explain why some juveniles become officially adjudicated. A number of self-report studies have been carried out, and it can now be determined whether there is any difference between official statistics and the findings of self-report surveys.

Austin Porterfield conducted the first self-report study ever attempted in 1946. He had 200 pre-college men, 130 pre-college women, and 100 college men anonymously report delinquent acts on a confidential questionnaire. He found the pre-college men to admit to an average of 18 offenses, the women admitted to an average of five offenses, and the college men admitted to an average of 11 offenses. Significantly, everyone admitted having committed at least one criminal act or status offense.

In 1947, Wallerstein and Wylie administered questionnaires to 1,020 adult men and 678 women which listed 49 criminal offenses. The men admitted to an average of 18 offenses and the women admitted to 11 offenses each. In this study, 99 percent of those responding admitted to one or more offenses.

A third study, conducted by Short and Nye in two high schools and also in a juvenile correctional facility, found that virtually everyone admitted to engaging in at least some delinquent behavior. Many other self-report studies have uncovered similar results.

In addition to showing how common delinquency really is, self-report studies have also provided an indication of what percentage of juvenile offenders are caught. Once we know this, we will know how representative arrest statistics are of all juvenile crime.

In 1966, Martin Gold administered a self-report questionnaire to a random sample of teenagers in Flint, Michigan. Of those admitting to crimes, only 16 percent were caught and 10 percent were booked by police. Studies conducted by Erickson and Empey uncovered similar results. They administered a self-report to 180 15-17 year-old boys. Fifty of these boys had never been to court, 30 had been adjudicated only once, 50 were recidivists (repeat offenders), and 50 were currently incarcerated in a juvenile institution for their offenses. Nearly every boy admitted to some of the 22 offenses surveyed and over 95 percent were undetected by authorities. Studies conducted elsewhere have uncovered similar results [For a review, see Hood and Sparks, 1970].

Comparisons of the findings of self-report surveys to official statistics also reveals information about the types of juveniles who engage in delinquency. Although official statistics indicate that males engage in delinquency at a rate of five to seven times that of females, self-reports have shown the actual rate of male offenses to be only about twice the female rate (depending on the crime). A national self-report survey by Ageton and Elliott found that females engage in petty larceny, drug use, and run away from home as often as males do. Males were found to engage in such offenses as joyriding, alcohol use, and truancy only twice as often as females.

Official statistics also indicate that delinquency is much

more common among juveniles of low socio-economic status than among middle-class juveniles (about 5 to 1). Self-report surveys, however, have found a variable mixture, and suggest that juvenile offenders from lower-class families are just as common as juvenile offenders from middle-class families. Lower-class juveniles, nevertheless, were found more likely to be chronic and serious offenders. In addition, official statistics indicate that most delinquents are non-white, but self-reports show that delinquency by white and black youths to be equally prevalent, although blacks appear to commit serious offenses more often [Elliott and Ageton, 1980].

This comparison between self-report and official data shows strikingly different conclusions about the nature of delinquency. Perhaps the most significant contribution of self-reports to our knowledge of delinquency is that they reveal that nearly all juveniles break the law at one time or another. Only a small proportion, however, engage in persistent or serious criminal behavior. Interestingly, only 10-20 percent of those who have committed offenses are caught and arrested, but official statistics contain a greater proportion of the most serious and frequent delinquents. Finally, self-reports have shown that sex, race, and social class are more equitably distributed among those committing delinquent acts than official statistics indicate.

THE TRUE EXTENT OF DELINQUENCY

Self-reports have shown that delinquency is far more common than official statistics would lead us to believe. Nevertheless, even the accuracy of self-reports has sometimes been questioned.

Two fundamental methodological questions have been identified in self-reports: validity (was the act really a crime?) and reliability (are many offenses concealed or exaggerated?). Self-report studies have been administered in two different ways to try to reduce the likelihood of these problems. The most common form of self-report is the check-list. A list of offenses is presented to the juvenile and he or she checks those acts that have been committed and how often. A second way to administer a self-report is through interviews where the juvenile is given a deck of cards with the description of an offense on each one. He or she is asked to sort the cards into two piles for those offenses committed and those not committed. The interviewer then asks the juvenile about the details of the incidents.

Questions of validity have arisen when the descriptions of offenses are very brief (such as "attacked another person causing him harm") and may not have constituted an offense given the circumstances in which it occurred. Further, juveniles of different social classes may perceive various acts differently. A "fight" might be an everyday occurrence for a lower-class youth, but it might constitute an assault for a middle-class youth.

Questions of reliability have arisen when poor reading ability, comprehension, or motivation exists while responding to a self-completion questionnaire. The possibility for exaggeration has been accounted for by re-testing juveniles after a certain period of time. If a respondent was exaggerating, it is extremely difficult to exaggerate in the same way each time. Concealment has also been examined by comparing self-reported crimes with police records (expecting to find more delinquency than official records indicate). Clark and Tift used this comparison, as well as a lie detector, to check the responses of 40 students. They found very little evidence of concealment. A third method of checking for concealment was attempted by Gold. He used associates of the juveniles in his study as "informants" to provide detailed information about the self-reported acts he uncovered, and other acts that they might have concealed. Similar to Clark and Tift, he found better than 80 percent of the offenses discovered were acknowledged in the self-report.

Perhaps the strongest evidence in support of the validity and reliability of self-reports is the similarity in findings among all studies that have been done. As described earlier, the fact that delinquency is a nearly universal experience is uncontested among the findings of self-reports.

In addition to self-reports, there exists still a third method that is used to measure the true extent of crime. Every year since 1973, a representative sample of the United States population is surveyed by the Bureau of the Census. People are asked whether or not they have been the victim of certain crimes (rape, robbery, assault, burglary, larceny, motor vehicle theft) during the past six months. The victimization surveys are then used to estimate the true extent of crime in the United States. A primary advantage of victim surveys is that they record all victimizations whether or not they have ben reported to the police. In addition, information about the incident is collected, providing much more information about criminal incidents than is provided by official statistics.

Unfortunately, victimization surveys have not been found to be very useful in the study of juvenile delinquency. This is because most delinquent acts are victimless crimes. Self-report studies have shown that juveniles most often commit crimes that involve voluntary participation of the victim and the offender, such as drug use, fornication, gambling, alcohol use, and prostitution. These crimes are not included in victimization surveys. For the property crimes that are included in victimization surveys, the age of the offender is often impossible to determine. The crimes of burglary, larceny, and motor vehicle theft involve only property as victims and, therefore, it is not possible to determine through victimization surveys who the offenders are. Furthermore, few victims of violent crimes can be positive about the age of the offender. Rape, robbery, and assault all involve personal confrontations, yet it is difficult for victims to know whether the offender was 15, 18, or 21 years old.

The most surprising finding of victimization surveys is that two to four times more crime occurs than is reported to police. In 1980, for example, less than 30 percent of all property crimes were reported to police, and less than 47 percent of all violent crimes were reported [Paez and Dodge, 1982]. Another important finding of victimization surveys is that the commonly offered notion that elderly persons suffer the greatest risk from serious crime is not true.

> The victimization rate for crimes of violence for people over 65 is about 8 per 1,000 versus 37 per 1,000 for those under 65. For the crime of personal theft, the rate os 23 per 1,000 for the elderly versus 104 per 1,000 for persons under 65. These findings contradict a common belief that the elderly are particularly prone to criminal victimization [Klaus, 1981].

As mentioned at the outset, the use of self-report instruments is very important in the investigation of juvenile delinquency. In addition to examining differences between "hidden" delinquents and adjudicated delinquents, self-reports help in developing explanations of delinquent behavior. Explanations of delinquency based on official statistics can be very misleading because they are based on only 10-20 percent of all delinquents (because only that percentage is ever caught). Self-reports are also useful in establishing programs to reduce delinquency. In order for a program to be successful it must address the true extent of delinquency and not merely reduce the number of juveniles who are caught and adjudicated. In subsequent chapters we will ultimately return to the prevention of delinquency, following a review of the explanations of and adjudication of juvenile law violators.

REFERENCES

Ageton, Suzanne S. and Elliott, Delbert S. The Incidence of Delinquent Behavior in a National Probability Sample. Boulder, Colorado: Behavioral Research Institute, 1978.

Clark, John P. and Tift, Larry L. Polygraph and Interview Validation of Self-Reported Deviant Behavior. American Sociological Review, 31 [1966], 516-523.

Cohen, Albert K. Delinquent Boys: The Culture of the Gang. New York: The Free Press, 1955.

Elliott, Delbert S. and Ageton, Suzanne S. Reconciling Race and Class Differences in Self Reported and Official Estimates of Delinquency. American Sociological Review, 45 [February, 1980], 95-110.

Erickson, Maynard L. and Empey, LaMar T. Court, Records, Undetected Delinquency and Decision Making. Journal of Criminal law, Criminology, and Police Science, 54 [1963], 456-469.

Gold, Martin. Undetected Delinquent Behavior. Journal of Research in Crime & Delinquency, 3 [1966], 27-46.

Hood, Roger and Sparks, Richard. Key Issues in Criminology. New York: McGraw-Hill, 1970.

Klaus, Patsy. Measuring Crime. Washington, D.C.: Bureau of Justice Statistics, 1981.

Klaus, Patsy. Victims of Crime. Washington, D.C.: Bureau of Justice Statistics, 1981.

Paez, Adolfo L. and Dodge, Richard W. Criminal Victimization in the United States. Washington, D.C.: Bureau of Justice

Statistics, 1982.

Porterfield, Austin L. Youth in Trouble. Fort Worth: Texas Christian University Press, 1946.

President's Commission on Law Enforcement and Administration of Justice. Task Force Report: Crime and Its Impact - An Assessment. Washington, D.C.: U.S. Government Printing Office, 1967.

Short, James F. and Nye, F. Ivan. Extent of Unrecorded Juvenile Delinquency. Journal of Criminal Law, Criminology, and Police Science, 49 [1958], 296-302.

U.S. Department of Justice. Federal Bureau of Investigation. Crime in the United States - Uniform Crime Reports. Washington, D.C.: U.S. Government Printing Office, Issued Annually.

Wallerstein, J.S. and Wylie, C.L. Our Law-abiding Lawbreakers. National Probation, [March-April, 1947], 107-112.

3. WHY DO JUVENILES MISBEHAVE?

CLASSICISM v. POSITIVISM

Equipped with an understanding of the true nature and extent of delinquency, we are still left without an understanding of why it occurs. As the preceding review of self-report studies has shown, nearly all juveniles engage in at least some delinquency. Therefore, theories of delinquency attempt to explain why some juveniles engage in persistent and serious criminal behavior, while others do not.

Before we talk about the causes of delinquent behavior, however, it is necessary to make an initial judgement about the causes of behavior in general. That is, what causes people to behave as they do?

There are essentially two schools of though regarding the causes of human behavior. According to the classical school, human behavior is rationa and a product of free-will. In this view, people are seen as rati nally choosing between alternate causes of co duct, usually in a way that will maximize pleasure and minimize pain. Cesare Beccaria and Jeremy Bentham are two of the best known classicists, and they helped to set forth the principles of classicism during the 1700s. As they saw it, all men are equal in their capacity to live by reason. Unfortunately, people are also naturally hedonistic and want to maximize pleasure and minimize pain. As a result, law and social control are necessary to restrain people from interfering with the fr edom of others. Without law, society could not exist, due to the co flicts that would arise in the pursuit of pleasure and minimization of pain.

Classical thinking, sometimes called the "free-will" school, dominated nearly all criminal codes throughout the 19th century. Because all men were equal in their capacity for rational conduct, the law treated all men equally and focused solely on the type of act committed. Therefore, punishment for a law violation was scaled accordin the type of act committed--the more serious the crime, the more severe the punishment. It was felt that if people realize what the punishment is for engaging in certain behaviors, they will be deterred from engaging in them. The punishment would increase pain beyond pleasure, so individuals would guide their freely-willed actions accordingly.

By the end of the 19th century, however, there was much

dissatisfaction with the classical school. Crime was still seen as an increasing problem, and punishment did not appear to deter criminal acts. In addition, this period saw the rise of social science and the scientific method, largely through the work of Charles Darwin and Emile Durkheim. Darwin catalogued variations in animal life and published them in Origin of Species in which he put forth his theory of evolution through natural selection, based on his observations. Emile Durkheim, a founder of sociology, examined variations in the rate of suicides in French provinces. Based on these observations, he developed explanations of why people commit suicide. In both cases, Darwin and Durkheim were pioneers in furthering scientific knowledge through observation. This approach gave rise to the positive school of criminology.

According to the positive school, human behavior is determined by internal and external influences. Rather than a person choosing between right and wrong, as classicists suggest, positivists maintain that biological, psychological, or social factors are what determine individual behavior. Unlike classical thought, positivism suggests that all men are not equal. That is, there are fundamental differences between criminals and non-criminals, based largely on hereditary and environmental factors. Cesare Lombroso was the pioneer of the positive school of criminology, and he offered one of the first empirically-based (based on observation) theories of why people commit crime.

BIOLOGICAL EXPLANATIONS

Lombroso (1835-1909) noticed that criminals often looked different from other people. He took body measurements of offenders in Italian prisons and concluded that there are "born criminals" with distinct bodily characteristics. His theory was based on the concept of atavism.

By his theory of atavism Lombroso meant that the "born criminal" was a biological throwback to an earlier stage of human evolution. As one might imagine, this notion of biological determinism had both its defenders and critics, a debate that was intensified because Darwin's theory of evolution was still relatively new.

In 1913, however, a physician, Charles Goring, published his measurements of 3,000 English convicts and also did measurements on a comparison group of non-convicts. He found no evidence of a distinct physical criminal type. Goring's study is still considered the definitive test in rejecting Lombroso's notion of atavism, but biologically-based explanations of delinquency continued.

In 1949, William Sheldon reported on the extensive physical measurements and background information he collected on 200 boys in a Boston reform school. Unlike Lombroso, Sheldon did not see atavism as the key in distinguishing criminals from non-criminals. Rather, he felt that basic body structure was linked to delinquency. Sheldon identified three basic body types: Mesomorphy (athletic, active, aggressive), Endomorphy (heavy, slow-moving, lethargic), and Ectomorphy (tall, thin, intellectual). He found mesomorphs to be the most predisposed to delinquency. Although he did not feel that mesomorphy caused delinquency, he felt it predisposed juveniles toward delinquency.

Sheldon concluded that, "whatever else may be true of the delinquency I saw in Boston, it is mainly in the germ plasm." Following Sheldon's view, the only really effective would be selective breeding to weed out the socially harmful types. Needless to say, Sheldon's notion of body-type and delinquency has been widely criticized on a number of points. Perhaps the most important criticism is his lack of clarity in explaining just how this body-type predisposes one to delinquency.

The Gluecks [1956] decided to test Sheldon's notion by comparing 500 identified delinquents with 500 non-delinquents in a controlled experiment. They found that body-type is not, in itself, a component of delinquent behavior. Rather, they found it to be only one of the many factors that may lead to delinquency. Even more importantly, the Gluecks pointed out that people tend to gravitate toward the occupations for which they are best able to succeed. As they concluded,

> We might well expect the athletic mesomorphs to
> be more attracted to delinquency than the
> roly-poly endomorphs and the skinny ectomorphs.

Still another test of Sheldon's hypothesis in 1972 by McCandless, Persons, and Roberts found no relationship between body-build and self-reported delinquency. As a result, there is little evidence to support Sheldon's explanation of delinquency.

Although Lombroso's and Sheldon's ideas regarding the biological link between body characteristics and delinquency have been fairly well discounted, other biological explanations have recently gained new-found prominence in the attempt to explain criminal behavior. Investigations of chromosomal abnormalities, glandular dysfunction, chemical imbalances, and nutritional deficiencies are examples of recent investigations in this area. While none of these have yet proved to be a satisfactory explanation of delinquent behavior, there is more and more research being done combing biological and environmental factors in an attempt to explain delinquency. Clearly, biological factors alone are not likely to be sufficient in explaining delinquency. As self-report studies have indicated, nearly all juveniles engage in some form of delinquent behavior, so biological abnormalities would have to be extremely common in order for them to fully explain delinquency. As LaMar Empey has recently concluded,

> The most objective conclusion would be that no final conclusions can be drawn. Nonetheless, we do know that, while efforts must be made to sort out the complex ways in which biological and environmental factors interact to produce human behavior, the prevalence of delinquent conduct is so great that we should not anticipate that biological factors alone will prove to be of overriding importance in explaining it [1982:170-1].

Nevertheless, it is doubtful that we have heard the last of biological explanations of delinquency.

PSYCHOLOGICAL EXPLANATIONS

Rather than looking at human physiology to explain delinquency, psychological approaches look at variations in the human psyche (or internalized controls). The oldest, and perhaps the most influential, psychological explanation of delinquency is the psychoanalytic instinct theory based on the work of Sigmund Freud (1856-1939). Psychoanalytic theory, according to Freud, is based on the interaction of the components of one's personality.

In Freud's view, there are three components to the personality: id, ego, and superego. The id is said to be the primitive instinctive drives that everyone is born with, such as aggression and sexual drives. The superego is the conscience, reflecting values developed through interaction with parents and significant others. The ego is said to mediate between the desires of the id and the values of the superego. Explanations of delinquency that are based on these three components of the personality focus on their interaction in affecting human conduct. Most of these theories explain delinquency in terms of faulty ego or superego structures which do not adequately control the id, resulting in personality imbalances that affect behavior.

Some psychological theories explain delinquency in terms of a weak or defective ego. That is to say, a person may be unable to manage the demands of the conscience while facing real life problems. This can result in guilt or in failure to resist temptation. An individual also may not be able to defer gratification or to stick to a single course of action. Literature on the role of the ego in deviance, however, is not extensive due to the ego's unclear role in many settings. Defects in the superego are much more commonly associated with deviant behavior.

In 1947, Richard Jenkins attempted to explain delinquency using Freud's notion of the structure of personality. Jenkins claimed that defects in the superego cause deviant behavior, and he identified three ways this might occur. Overinhibited individuals are those with an excessive development of the superego which can result in neurotic behavior and anxiety attacks. Unsocialized aggressives are, according to Jenkins, individuals with inadequate development of the superego. This type of person would exhibit insufficient control of his or her impulses and may be aggressive, showing little conscience. Socialized delinquents are individuals displaying normal superego inhibitions toward an accepted group or gang, but would not show superego controls toward an out-group. Individuals demonstrating violent or aggressive behavior toward certain people, but not others, would be an example of this phenomenon.

In additions to Sheldon's explanation of delinquency, there exist other explanations also based on the work of Freud. The psychopathic personality is said to be the failure of the superego to develop at all, leaving the juvenile devoid of a moral responsibility. Most psychologists and psychiatrists, who are proponents of these theories, agree that failure of the ego and superego to develop normally is the result of inadequate role models for children during early childhood. The ego and superego are said to develop during the years from birth to age six or seven, and it is believed by some psychologists that any damage is very difficult, if not impossible, to correct when appropriate parental relationships are not established during this period [McCord and McCord, 1956].

A second type of psychological theory of delinquency is based on defense mechanisms. Rather than a deviant impulse (id) breaking through the controls (ego or superego), theories based on defense mechanisms look at another type of internal process. Defense mechanisms take effect when an impulse (deviant or not) runs counter to the conscience, producing anxiety or guilt. By altering one's behavior it becomes possible to neutralize the anxiety or guilt.

There are three different types of defense mechanisms: displacement, unconsciously intended side effects, and reaction-formation. Displacement (or substitution) neutralizes anxiety that would normally result by substituting another target that, unconsciously, means the same thing to the person as the intended target. An example might be the unhappy employee who goes home each night and hits his spouse (who unconsciously substitutes for the employer). Unconsciously intended side effects occur when a person cannot admit a motive to himself, so an act is committed in a way that makes it look as if he had another motive. A juvenile might commit an overt delinquent act, for example, in order to invite punishment. Such an act may relieve guilt about an undetected act or desire. Finally, reaction-formation involves the denial of an unacceptable part of one's personality through behavior that appears to indicate the opposite. An example might be the display of "macho" type behavior as a reaction-formation against homosexual tendencies [Cohen, 1966].

None of these defense mechanisms, however, necessarily leads to delinquent behavior. Delinquency provides only one of a number of alternative solutions. A juvenile might become very generous, for example, as a reaction-formation against an unconscious desire to be greedy. On the other hand, he may also covertly steal merchandise.

Both the Freudian-based theories and those based on defense mechanisms have limitations common to all psychological theories. First, as self-reports have indicated, delinquency is so common that it is unlikely that internal personality imbalances are as widespread. Second, most delinquents do not become adult criminals. Psychological theories have difficulty explaining this. That is, how do these personality characteristics go away? Third, psychological explanations of delinquency pose the inherent dangers of tautology. That is, by attributing behavior to an unconscious or to a defective superego (neither of which is empirically verifiable), you are actually explaining behavior in terms of something unexplainable. Finally, psychological theories have difficulty explaining why juveniles choose a delinquent solution to personality conflicts, rather than a non-delinquent alternative. Neither a defective superego or a defense mechanism necessarily results in delinquent behavior. An adequate theory should be able to account for why this occurs in some cases, but not in others.

Similar to the biological explanations of delinquency, the psychological explanations have not performed well in practice. Schuessler and Cressey reviewed all studies of the personality characteristics of criminals up to 1950. Of the 113 studies reviewed, less than half found any significant difference between delinquent and non-delinquent personalities. In 1967, Waldo and Dinitz reviewed all studies conducted between 1950 and 1965. Of the 94 studies reviewed, they found little evidence that personality traits could predict delinquent involvement. Furthermore, like the biological studies, they found many research weaknesses such as the failure to control for environmental influences, the selection of non-random samples, and vagueness in the definitions of the traits they were measuring. Finally, in 1977, Tannenbaum reviewed personality studies from 1966 to 1975. He found that "personality tests, per se, are no better predictors of criminal personalities than were those of ten years ago...most results are based on tautological argument."

Although psychological theories of delinquency have not satisfactorily explained it, they have provided useful concepts to explain sometimes unexplainable behavior. As will be seen in the next section, psychological theories show somewhat greater success when they account for environmental influences as well.

SOCIOLOGICAL EXPLANATIONS

Sociological explanations of delinquency are more common than any other type. They arose largely from the inability of biological and psychological explanations to account for many types of delinquency. That is to say, many cases of delinquency appear to be normal reactions of people placed in bad social situations.

Unlike biological or psychological explanations, which look at some problem within the individual (whether physiological abnormalities or personality conflicts), the sociologist looks at environmental influences that affect the way people behave. One of the earliest attempts to explain juvenile delinquency from the sociological perspective was conducted by Clifford Shaw and Henry McKay.

Shaw and McKay looked at a map of the City of Chicago and noted which areas of town had high rates of delinquency and which had low rates. Interestingly, they noticed that the areas of the city with high delinquency rates in 1900-1906 were the sames areas with the highest rates in 1917-1923, even though the population of the area had completely changed. After an examination of the juvenile court records of nearly 25,000 juveniles, Shaw and McKay concluded that there were differences in social values between the high and low delinquency areas. They noticed that distinct ecological areas had developed in the city that could be grouped into concentric zones. They concluded that in the high-crime areas delinquency had becomes, "more or less traditional aspects of social life," and that "those traditions are transmitted through personal and group contacts."

Shaw and McKay found the high delinquency areas to possess conflicting moral values, social disorganization, and decaying transitional neighborhoods. Whereas the low delinquency areas were characterized by universal, conventional values and child-rearing practices. Furthermore, they believed the chief agencies for the transmission of delinquency was play-groups and gangs, because they found that most delinquent acts were committed in groups of two or three juveniles.

This view of delinquency is very different from the psychological approaches. As Shaw and McKay note,

> The human motives and desires underlying the boys' participation in the activities of his group are perhaps identical in the two neighborhood situations [of high and low delinquency].

Therefore, according to Shaw and McKay, the factors that

distinguish high and low delinquency areas are the "standards and values" of the people in those areas. In this environment, teenage gangs develop as a means of survival, friendship, and financial gain. When these groups recruit new members, the values and traditions are passed to the next generation. This process is called <u>cultural transmission</u>. Shaw and McKay felt this was the reason why the high delinquency areas remained the same over the years.

Perhaps the most important contribution of Shaw and mcKay's explanation of delinquency is their recognition of the importance of the ecology of the city in delinquent behavior. Another significant contribution they make is their point that delinquent gang membership may be a normal response to social conditions in slum areas. This is very different from the psychological approach which sees troubled personalities as the cause of delinquency. Two drawbacks to Shaw and McKay's notion of cultural transmission are: (1) They rely on police and court records to measure delinquency, and (2) They do not attempt to account for relatively high rates of delinquency in some suburban areas. As self-reports have shown, delinquency is far more common than official statistics indicate, and it is not confined to the socially or culturally deprived.

In 1938, a second important contribution to the understanding of delinquency was made by Robert Merton. Merton based his explanation of the concept of <u>anomie</u>. The notion of anomie was conceived by Emile Durkheim in the late 1800s. Durkheim, however, did not use anomie to explain delinquency in any systematic way. Rather, he used it to explain "pathological" forms of the division of labor in society and to explain suicide. Durkheim defined anomie as "normlessness" or when the common rules which regulate the relations among people in society have broken down. What Merton did was to separate out the components of anomie implied by Durkheim.

Merton identified three elements of modern society that sometimes interact to cause anomie: culture goals, norms, and institutionalized means. Culture goals are the goals of society that are internalized by its members and become their also. Being able to earn a living wage and having a family are examples of culture goals. Norms are the legitimate means by which people can pursue these culture goals. That is, a good education and a steady job are legitimate ways to achieve a living wage. Finally, the institutionalized means are the actual distribution of opportunities to achieve culture goals in a manner compatible with the means. Unequal employment opportunities, or the inability to afford a college education would be examples of inequality in the institutionalized means to achieve culture goals.

According to Merton, deviance does not depend on any one of these three elements but, rather, on the relationship among them. Changes in the goals (upward) or a reduction in the legitimate means to obtain them, or a change in the distribution of opportunities, may all upset the balance among them. According to Merton, the strain (or frustration) produced by any imbalance will weaken a person's commitment to the culture goals or institutionalized means, resulting in a state of anomie.

Merton went on to develop a scheme of logically possible ways by which a person might adapt to this strain caused by the social structure. That is, a person may either accept or reject the culture goals, or he might accept or reject the institutionalized means. Either choice was seen as ultimately affecting a person's behavior. In Merton's view. a conformist is one who accepts both the culture goals and the institutionalized means. An innovator would be one who accepts the culture goals but rejects the institutionalized means, A ritualist rejects the culture goals but accepts the institutionalized means, and rebellion occurs when someone rejects both the goals and means, but substitutes new ones in their place.

The most important contribution of Merton's theory of anomie is that he does not confine deviance to one particular social class or to a personality conflict. On the other hand, its most significant limitation is that the theory provides no clue as to what causes a person to choose one adaptation over another in response to social strain. It can be seen that explanations of delinquency are becoming more sophisticated during this period, and they are better able to account for the varied circumstances that might lead to delinquency.

In 1939, Edwin Sutherland formulated perhaps the most influential theory of delinquency yet devised. Sutherland felt that delinquent behavior is learned, much in the same way a person learns anything else. This process is called differential association and refers to the process by which a person becomes criminal or delinquent when definitions favorable to law violation exceed definitions unfavorable to law violation. According to Sutherland, these definitions are learned from intimate personal groups such as family, friends, or peers. Although everybody is exposed to pro-criminal and anti-criminal definitions, the proportion one receives of one or the other is central to differential association. Therefore, Sutherland does not speak of associations with criminals or non-criminals but, rather, with definitions favorable to crime. Although a juvenile may not associate with many delinquents, his associations may still expose him to pro-criminal definitions.

Sutherland's theory is a general theory inasmuch as it attempts to present a framework for understanding delinquency. Although a number of different factors such as poverty, criminal associates, family situation, or drug use may sometimes be associated with crime, they do not provide a clue as to how or why they are related. What differential association attempts to do is provide the link between the various correlates of criminality. This is perhaps the greatest strength of differential association theory. Using the concept of learning, its shows the similarity of criminal behavior to other types of behavior.

Several researchers have investigated the link between juvenile associations and delinquency in order to determine how well differential association explains juvenile crime. Unfortunately, the results are mixed, finding it to be a better explanation of the spread of delinquency rather than its ultimate cause (i.e., where does the first person obtain definitions favorable to crime?). Also, it has been found to be difficult to adequately measure an "excess of favorable definitions toward crime." This lack of clarity in explanatory terms has also contributed to the uneven support found by empirical investigations of the explanato y power of differential association [Reiss and Rhodes, 1961; Hirschi, 1969].

After Sutherland, the next major sociological theory of delinquency was developed by Albert Cohen in 1955. In his book, Delinquent Boys, Cohen attempted to explain senseless, purely negative acts that have no apparent purpose. Pointless acts are probably not learned (such as wanton vandalism), so a mechanism other than differential association must explain these apparently irrational acts.

Cohen felt that a person's self-image depends upon how you are judged by others. If people around you have a low opinion of you, you are likely to have a low opinion of yourself. In addition, the majority of people who judge you are from the middle class (e.g., teachers, employers, the media), who set middle-class standards or "measuring rods" for juveniles to live up to. Therefore, young people of different social classes, races, and ethnicity are competing with one another for status and approval.

The problem with this situation is that all juveniles are not equally equipped to be successful in attaining the same middle-class goals. As a result, lower-class juveniles are more likely to experience failure and frustration in attaining these goals than are middle- and upper-class juveniles. Cohen called this situation "status-frustration."

Cohen claims that juveniles resolve this status-frustration by reaction-formation through which middle-class values and norms are replaced by their own subcultural values. Therefore, lower-class juveniles gain status through behavior they can achieve by turning existing values upside down and engaging in negative behavior for their own, short-run gratification. Thus, the delinquent subculture provides a group solution for all those juveniles suffering from status-frustration.

Like Sutherland, Merton, and Shaw and McKay, Cohen's explanation is a sociological theory because its causal assumptions are based in social conditions. Cohen's theory is somewhat different, however, because he shows how a social condition may trigger a psychological defense mechanism (reaction-formation). His theory is important because it provides a systematic way to explain seemingly senseless delinquent acts. However, Cohen's theory is difficult to test because of its reliance on an unmeasurable psychological defense mechanism. Also, it does not explain the widespread delinquency of middle-class juveniles who do not experience status-frustration [Kitsuse and Detrick, 1959].

In 1958, an anthropologist, Walter Miller, took a somewhat different approach in explaining delinquency. He studied delinquent gangs in a major eastern city and found that slum areas have distinct cultural values that remain stable over time. Miller felt these areas are on the fringe of the economic system and that these people have little chance for success in the social and economic mainstream. As a result, they have their own goals and culture.

Miller saw delinquency as a product consistent with the values and attitudes of lower-class culture, unlike Shaw and McKay who felt that delinquent traditions arose from unsupervised play-groups. According to Miller, lower-class boys are often brought up in female-dominated households, so the street corner gang

> ...provides the first real opportunity to learn essential aspects of the male role in the context of peers facing similar problems of sex-role identification.

Furthermore, Miller saw the peer group as "the most stable and solidary primary group he [the juvenile] has ever belonged to." By reinforcing lower-class cultural values and norms (which are different from conventional society and include, for example, toughness, excitement, freedom from authority, cleverness, and belonging to groups), Miller sees the influence of the peer group as the mechanism by which adolescents become delinquent.

The most important contribution of Miller's theory is its suggestion that delinquency does not necessarily arise from conflict with conventional society, but it may simply be an accepted behavior in a stable lower-class culture. However, some empirical investigations have shown that many lower-class delinquents actually share many of the values of non-delinquents [Siegel, Rathus, and Ruppert, 1973].

The 1960s saw the development of four of the most recent recent explanations of delinquency. In 1960, Richard Cloward and Lloyd Ohlin published a book titled, Delinquency and Opportunity. As students of Robert merton, they agreed with his claim that delinquency results from lack of access to legitimate means for achieving social goals. However, Cloward and Ohlin felt that even illegitimate means are unevenly distributed in society. As a result, some lower-class neighborhoods provide greater opportunity for illegal gain than do others. Cloward and Ohlin also claimed that there is greater opportunity to get ahead through illegitimate means in middle- or upper-class areas. In low income areas, however, legitimate means are harder to come by and juveniles often seek illegitimate avenues of success.

The approach of Cloward and Ohlin is different from that of Cohen because Cohen maintains that the lower-class youths cannot meet and, therefore, reject middle-class values and substitute their own. According to Cloward and Ohlin, however, youths do not substitute new values, but they merely use illegitimate means to obtain accepted societal goals. Furthermore, Cloward and Ohlin believe that not all delinquents can achieve success through illegitimate means because there is a differential opportunity structure to obtain societal goals by illegitimate means, just as there is to obtain these goals by legitimate means.

Cloward and Ohlin describe three types of criminal subcultures that develop when youths withdraw legitimacy from middle-class standards. Youths may become part of the adult "criminal" subculture, they may participate in the "conflict" subculture by forming fighting gangs that emphasize violence and status by coercion, or they may become part of the "retreatist" subculture when either no opportunities exist in the criminal subculture or status cannot be obtained in the conflict group. Therefore, Cloward and Ohlin maintain that not only legitimate opportunities for success are blocked for lower-class juveniles, but illegitimate opportunities can also be blocked, resulting in one of these types of delinquent subculture.

Cloward and Ohlin's opportunity theory is a broad theory which accounts for several types of delinquency. It also provides a clear direction for delinquency prevention programs which will be discussed in Chapter 8. Their theory fails to account, however, for the relatively widespread middle-class delinquency revealed by self-reports.

Sociologist Howard Becker popularized labelling theory in his 1963 book, The Outsiders. Originally put forth in 1951 by Edwin Lemert, labelling theory holds that "when society acts negatively to a particular individual (through adjudication), by means of the 'label' (delinquent)--we actually encourage future delinquency." So for Lemert and Becker, the labelling process depends less on the behavior of the delinquent than it does on the way others view their acts. It is society's labelling of the individual (through adjudication as a delinquent) that promotes deviant behavior, rather than any action or thought process by the juvenile.

The labelling perspective is enhanced by two facts: (1) Total delinquency does not exist, and (2) Definitions of deviance change over time and from place to place.

According to Becker, delinquents and non-delinquents are really quite similar, and the juvenile who is not caught and adjudicated will probably not continue in his deviant behavior. However, juveniles adjudicated as delinquents, either through a negative public identity or through a changed self-image, are actually encouraged to commit future acts of delinquency. So the more frequent and prolonged the contacts are with the juvenile justice system, the more likely it is that an offender will ultimately accept the delinquent label as a personal identity and perhaps enter into a life of crime.

Labelling theory has had a significant impact in its recognition that the effect of the adjudication process may make behavior worse, rather than prevent it in the future. As comparisons of self-reports and official statistics have indicated, those delinquents who are caught tend to be the more frequent and serious offenders and are often those who have been caught before. On the other hand, empirical evidence is mixed regarding the effect of adjudication on a juvenile's self-image [Davis, 1972].

Holding assumptions similar to those of Becker, David Matza published a book in 1964 titled, Delinquency and Drift, which was based on earlier work he had done with Gresham Sykes. Like Becker, Matza did not feel that there exists a lower-class delinquency subculture. He claimed that delinquents hold attitudes similar to those of law-abiding citizens.

Matza established three propositions to support his assumptions. First, most delinquents realize that what they do is wrong and feel guilty about it. They learn "techniques of neutralization" to rationalize it, claiming the behavior was necessary in self-defense or that the victim deserved it. Second, a full-fledged delinquent subculture that causes juveniles to commit crime is unrealistic. Juveniles are not committed to full-time conflict with society. Matza believes that delinquency is episodic and that juveniles "drift" away from the rules of society (through neutralization techniques), but that they also drift back. Finally, delinquency is easily given up. As statistics indicate, most juveniles commit crimes, but they generally do not become adult criminals. Proponents of a delinquent subculture have difficulty explaining this.

Matza argues that delinquency occurs because adolescents are in a state of suspension between childhood and adulthood. They spend alot of time with their peers and are anxious for their acceptance. He describes peer-group pressure to commit crime as a "comedy of errors," where each group member believes everyone else is committed to delinquency, so he supports it. But, in fact, the rest of the group is not committed to delinquency either. They are all victims of "shared misunderstandings."

Matza's explanation of delinquency is important in that it accounts for the fact that most juveniles do not become adult criminals. However, it does not explain why some juveniles drift into delinquency more than others.

A final sociological explanation of delinquency was put forth by Travis Hirschi in his 1969 book, Causes of Delinquency. Hirschi linked delinquent behavior to the bond an individual has to society. When the bond is weak, or breaks, the constraints that society places on you are weakened or broken. As a result, you are more likely to break the law.

Hirschi assumes that everyone is a potential delinquent, and that social controls are needed to maintain order. According to Hirschi, a person's social bond to society has four primary elements: attachment to others, commitment to conventional activities, involvement in conventional activities, and belief in widely shared moral values.

In an attempt to test his theory, Hirschi administered a self-report survey to 4,000 junior and senior high school students in California. He found that strong attachments to parents, commitment to values, involvement in school, and respect for police and law, reduced the likelihood of delinquency. A replication of this study in Albany, New York generally supported Hirschi's results [Hindelang, 1973].

Hirschi's explanation of delinquency is very significant because it is not limited to any particular social class, and it also has empirical support. It fails to describe, however, the chain of events or factors that weaken the elements of the social bond. Nevertheless, Hirschi's theory remains influential in the explanation of delinquency.

SUMMARIZING EXPERIENCE

As this review of explanations of juvenile delinquency has indicated, there have been many efforts made in an attempt

Table 1.   SOCIOLOGICAL THEORIES OF DELINQUENCY

Founder	Causal Assumptions	Motivational Mechanism	Deviant Outcome
Shaw & McKay [1932]	Social disorganization & conflicting moral values in transitional neighborhoods.	Cultural Transmission	Delinquency becomes a traditional aspect of social life.
Merton [1938]	Disjunction between culture goals and institutionalized means in society.	Strain	Anomie (weakened attachment to goals & means)
Sutherland [1939]	Criminal behavior is learned	Differential Association	Excess definitions favorable to crime
Cohen [1955]	Lower-class males cannot attain middle-class goals (status-frustration)	Reaction-Formation	Replace middle-values with sub-cultural values.
Miller [1958]	Lower class has different values from middle class.	Peer group solidarity & influence	Reinforced lower-class values toward delinquency.
Cloward & Ohlin [1960]	Lower-class males face blocked opportunity for legitimate advancement.	Withdrawal of legitimacy from middle-class goals.	1. Criminal 2. Conflict 3. Retreatist Subculture
Becker [1963] Lemert [1951]	Delinquents and non-delinquents are really quite similar.	Deviant label (through adjudication)	Further delinquency is encouraged by negative public identity or changed self-image.
Matza [1964]	Delinquency is episodic & more similarity than difference between delinquents & non-delinquents.	Maintenance of status within peer group through techniques of neutralization	Youths "drift" in & out of delinquency. Not committed to full-time conflict with conventional society.
Hirschi [1969]	All juveniles are potential delinquents held in check by social controls (attachment, commitment, involvement and belief)	Weakening of social bond to society	Rejection of social norms and beliefs.

to understand why some juveniles violate the law persistently and seriously. Having summarized two biological explanations, two psychological explanations, and nine sociological explanations, it is clear that most efforts to explain delinquency are based on social influences. Although none of the nine theories presented here adequately explain all delinquency, many of them offer satisfactory answers for the delinquency of at least some youth. It remains for further empirical investigations to test and reformulate these explanations, so that future work will be able to more adequately account for the delinquency of a greater number of juveniles.

In order to facilitate comparisons among the theories described above, Table 1 provides brief summarizes of the more important elements of each sociological explanation. Every theory, including biological and psychological approaches, can be broken down into three component parts. Each author makes causal assumptions about the behavior he attempts to explain, and he also refers to specific types of deviant outcomes that he is explaining. The central part of any theory, however, is the motivational mechanism that links the assumptions to the deviant outcome. Most theories are remembered by the nature of the mechanism involved. In the next chapter, we will begin a review of the juvenile justice system in acting upon juveniles whose delinquency has been detected by the authorities.

REFERENCES

Beccaria, Cesare. Essay on Crimes and Punishments. [1764]. New York: Bobbs-Merrill, 1963.

Becker, Howard. The Outsiders: Studies in the Sociology of Deviance. New York: Free Press, 1963.

Cloward, Richard and Ohlin, Lloyd. Delinquency and Opportunity. New York: Free Press, 1960.

Cohen, Albert K. Delinquent Boys: The Culture of the Gang. [1955]. New York: Free Press, 1971.

Darwin, Charles. Origin of Species. [1871]. New York: Modern Library, 1936.

Davis, Nanette. Labelling Theory in Deviance Research: A Critique and Reconsideration. Sociological Quarterly, 13 [1972], 447-474.

Durkheim, Emile. *Suicide*. [1890]. New York: Free Press, 1951.

Empey, LaMar T. *American Delinquency: Its Meaning and Construction*. [Revised Edition]. Homewood, Ill.: Dorsey Press, 1982.

Glueck, Sheldon and Glueck, Eleanor. *Physique and Delinquency*. New York: Harper, 1956.

Goring, Charles. *The English Convict*. London: Her Majesty's Stationery Office, 1913.

Hindelang, Michael J. Causes of Delinquency: A Partial Replication and Extension. *Social Problems*, 20 [1973], 470-487.

Hirschi, Travis. *Causes of Delinquency*. Berkeley: University of California Press, 1969.

Jenkins, Richard and Hewitt, Lester F. *Fundamental Patterns of Maladjustment*. Springfield, Ill.: Thomas, 1947.

Kitsuse, John and Detrick, David. Delinquent Boys: A Critique. *American Sociological Review*, 24 [1959], 208-215.

Lemert, Edwin M. *Social Pathology: A Systematic Approach to the Theory of Sociopathic Behavior*. New York: McGraw-Hill, 1951.

Lombroso, Cesare and Lombroso-Ferrero, Gina. *The Criminal Man*. Montclair, N.J.: Patterson-Smith, 1972.

Matza, David. *Delinquency and Drift*. New York: Wiley, 1964.

McCandless, B.R., Persons, W.S., and Roberts, A. Perceived Opportunity, Delinquency, Race, and Body Build Among Delinquent Youth. *Journal of Consulting and Clinical Psychology*, 38 [1972], 281.

McCord, William and McCord, Joan. *Psychopathy and Delinquency*. New York: Grune & Stratton, 1956.

Miller, Walter. Lower Class Culture as a Generating Milieu of Gang Delinquency. *Journal of Social Issues*, 14 [1958], 5-19.

Reiss, Albert and Rhodes, A. Lewis. The Distribution of Delinquency in the Social Class Structure. American Sociological Review, 26 [1961], 732.

Schuessler, Karl and Cressey, Donald. Personality Characteristics of Criminals. American Journal of Sociology, 55 [1950], 476-484.

Shaw, Clifford R. and Henry D. McKay. Juvenile Delinquency and Urban Areas. [1932]. Chicago: University of Chicago Press, 1969.

Sheldon, William H. Varieties of Delinquent Youth. New York: Harper, 1949.

Siegel, Larry, Rathus, Spencer, and Ruppert, Carol. Values and Delinquent Youth: An Empirical Reexamination of Theories of Delinquency. British Journal of Criminology, 6 [1973], 135-140.

Sutherland, Edwin H. Principles of Criminology. Philadelphia: Lippincott, 1939.

Sykes, Gresham M. and Matza, David. Techniques of Neutralization: A Theory of Delinquency. American Sociological Review, 22 [1957], 664-670.

Tannenbaum, David J. Personality and Criminality: A Summary and Implications of the Literature. Journal of Criminal Justice, 5 [1977], 225-235.

Waldo, Gordon and Dinitz, Simon. Personality Attributes of the Criminal: An Analysis of Research Studies: 1950-1965. Journal of Research in Crime & Delinquency, 4 [1967], 185-201.

4. WHY TREAT JUVENILES & ADULTS DIFFERENTLY ?

A SYSTEM OF JUSTICE

Let us assume that you have the opportunity to form a new country on an uninhabited island. Before you know it, there are several thousand people on your island, and you are starting to get some serious complaints. You are hearing disputes over property rights, reports of thefts, quarreling, and even a few fist fights.

After a few months of this, the residents of your island community are becoming dissatisfied with your decisions in these cases and demand a democratic and impartial system for settling these disputes. In effect, you are being asked to set up a justice system.

As you attempt to do this, you face some fundamental questions that must be answered. What should the goal of the system be? Merely fairness? Deterrence of future misbehavior? Reformation of rule violators?

If you are going to set up a system of adjudication, you will also have to be specific about its jurisdiction. Over what types of acts will the justice system have authority? As a result, it will be necessary to codify behaviors that are subject to adjudication. Those actions that threaten the social order will probably be grouped in a criminal code.

The next question that arises is how broad or narrow do you wish to make the code? It is likely that crimes of assault (murder, rape, robbery) will be included, as will crimes of theft (burglary, larceny, motor vehicle theft). But will you include acts that involve voluntary participation by the victim and offender, such as prostitution, gambling, or drug use? Will you include status offenses such as runaways or truancy? These are difficult decisions that are ultimately left up to legislators in a democratic society who act on behalf of the community they represent.

Once the criminal code is established, however, it will not be self-enforcing. Who will make sure that all people in your country abide by the code of behavior? Once a society reaches a size where self-protection is no longer feasible, the legislature will establish an agency of law enforcement to apprehend law violators. But then, additional questions will arise. How much authority should you give the law enforcement agency? When may they encroach upon private property? When may they search a person? How do you best balance the enforcement of the code with the rights of individuals? These are questions that are still being answered in the United States today through court decisions and new legislation.

Let us assume that you manage to resolve these dilemmas. What happens when the law enforcement people catch a suspected code violator? Can the person be put in jail prior to a judgement against him? How positive must you be before you can treat a suspected law violator as an offender: reasonably sure, somewhat convinced, absolutely positive? If, through your adjudication process, you find a person guilty of the violation alleged, on what basis do you sanction him? Retribution? Incapacitation? Deterrence? Reformation?

As you can see, the establishment of a system of justice arises out of necessity in a country, simply because not all people will agree on accepted forms of conduct in a society. Once a system is established, however, the procedures for dealing with code violators must address issues of purpose, privacy, fairness, and justice--issues that do not always have easy answers.

A DIFFERENCE IN RESPONSIBILITY

Let us assume that, as time goes on, you feel that younger citizens in your country ought to be treated differently than older citizens in the justice process. That is, you believe that adults are (and should be) more responsible for their actions than juveniles and, therefore, should be treated differently. This is the conclusion that was reached in the United States when the first juvenile court was established in 1899.

As Table 1 indicates, the juvenile justice system uses different terminology than the adult system, illustrating the difference in philosophy. The juvenile justice system has more neutral terminology, whereas the adult system is an adversary system with formal accusations and convictions.

The establishment of the juvenile court corresponded with the rise of positivism which saw crimes as the product of internal or external influences, rather than the result of free-will.

Table 1. Adult & Juvenile Justice System Terminology.

Procedure	Juvenile	Adult
Act	Delinquency	Crime
Apprehension	Take into Custody Petition	Arrest Indictment
Pre-Adjudication	Detention Agree to finding Deny the petition	Jail Plead Guilty Plead not guilty
Adjudication	Adjudicatory Hearing Adjudicated Delinquent	Trial Convicted Criminal
Corrections	Disposition Hearing Disposition Commitment	Sentencing Sentence Incarceration

Logically, what is seen as the fundamental cause of human behavior will be reflected in the systems established to deal with it. If juvenile delinquency is seen as the result of environmental influences, for example, a justice process will attempt to correct the influences, or to correct the way the juvenile responds to these influences. On the other hand, if crime is seen as the product of one's free will, the only logical way to deal with it is through punishment to deter future misbehavior. In this way, people will guide their freely-willed actions accordingly. Unfortunately, prevailing views regarding the responsibility and treatment of juveniles have shifted over the years.

THREE MODELS OF JUVENILE JUSTICE

Currently, there is much disagreement over the proper goals of the juvenile justice system. This disagreement can be traced to the philosophical differences between the classical and positive schools of criminology. For example, it is often said that the United States must concentrate more fully on "law and order," which usually suggests the view that society needs to be protected from criminals. From another constituency, it is often said that we have to do our best to make law violators, especially juvenile delinquents, into "productive citizens." This usually indicates the view that criminals have problems that society should seek to correct. Still a third group claims that individual freedoms should be protected at all costs. Governments exist at the pleasure of the people, and the ability of the government to interfere in the lives of its citizens should be severely restricted. This focus on "individual protections" reflects the view that citizens must be adequately protected from the arbitrary exercise of governmental power.

It is probably true that everyone gives at least some credence to each of these three perspectives. Nevertheless, we usually see one view as being more important than the others. Depending upon what you see as the overriding goal of juvenile justice, this "philosophy" will be reflected in your view of a properly functioning juvenile justice system.

Table 2 represents how the juvenile justice system would work under each of the primary goals of law and order, productive citizens, and individual protections. The crime control model represents the law and order view. According to this model, the rights of the commun ty are paramount with efficiency important to repress crime. Also, there would be a presumption of guilt for those reaching the adjudicatory stage because more weight would be placed on police decisions. Following the classical view, the punishment would fit the crime, assuming that all men are equal in their ability to choose among alternate courses of conduct.

The rehabilitative model places the needs of the individual as a paramount concern, and the justice system is based on a presumption of need. Following the positivistic view that delinquency results from internal or external influences, the juvenile would be treated according to the type of problem he or she manifested. Unlike the crime control model, the act itself would not be of great importance because it is only a symptom of some underlying problem that needs to be addressed.

The due process model is based on a presumption of innocence and places the rights of the individual as an overriding concern. in dealing with delinquency. Unlike the crime control model, accuracy and fairness are seen as being much more important than efficiency. The trial or adjudicatory hearing would be the most important part of the process because it is at this stage where the protection of

Table 2. Models of Juvenile Justice.

	LAW	POLICE	DETENTION	ADJUDICATION	DISPOSITION
CRIME CONTROL GOAL Increase efficiency in screening suspects, determining guilt, & dispositions to repress criminal behavior.	Legal definition of delinquency broad. Behavior seen as leading to delinquency should be adjudicated.	Increased power to search, arrest, and interrogate. Arrest decision would be considered correct for most part.	Would be extensively used to incapacitate juveniles so they could not commit other crimes while awaiting adjudication.	Relatively unimportant. Swift resolution of cases necessary to minimize delay. Assumption of efficient police work.	Punishment would fit crime rather than offender. Goal to reduce crime through incapacitation and deterrence.
REHABILITATIVE GOAL "Guilt" not relevant because juvs cannot be held fully responsible. Delinquency is a symptom of underlying problems to be addressed by juv. justice sys.	Legal definition of delinquency broad. Harmful behaviors may indicate underlying social or psychological problems.	Police would have juvenile specialists trained in psy and social diagnosis and treatment to identify problems early.	Would not be used very often, only in cases where juvenile needs protection or special care.	Guilt or innocence not very important. Focus on juv's psychological and social condition. Informal hearing designed to help juvenile.	Juvenile would be placed in once of a wide range of programs based on psychological or social needs (Not according to particular act committed)
DUE PROCESS GOAL Accuracy & fairness more important than efficiency. Gov't must be limited in ability to accuse citizens of crime & to deny one's civil liberties via adjudication	Legal definition of delinquency narrow. Vague or ambiguous definitions eliminated. Status offenses eliminated.	Police arrests, searches, and interrogations would be carefully reviewed to prevent abuses of power and of individual rights.	Not extensively used. Detention only employed with careful attention to individual rights. Hearing would be required.	Trial most important part of process to insure accuracy of facts and fairness in proceeding against defendant by the govt	Not so much concerned with content or rationale for penalty as with fairness in decisionmaking process. Unequal sentences not tolerated.

individual rights and the accuracy of the allegations of misconduct can be most closely scrutinized.

These three models of alternative justice systems illustrate how one's philosophy of justice lies at the foundation of any justice syste . A society's assumptions regarding the causes of misconduct and the relationship between the individual and his government translate into the procedure by which those accused of crimes are treated. This distinction among the three models of justice will become increasingly significant in subsequent chapters when we will see that the rehabilitative model, based on positivism, formed the philosophy of juvenile court procedure from its inception until the 1960s. Evidence will be provide to show that a due process emphasis became apparent during the 1960s through the mid-1970s. Finally, recent events in juvenile justice will illustrate a contemporary trend toward the crime control model during the last 10 years.

REFERENCES

Faust, Frederic L. and Brantingham, Paul J. Models of Juvenile Justice: Introduction and Overview. In Juvenile Justice Philosophy. [Second Edition]. St Paul, Minn.: West Publishing, 1979.

Packer, Herbert L. The Limits of the Criminal Sanction. Stanford, Ca.: Stanford University Press, 1968.

5. HOW DOES A JUVENILE ENTER THE JUSTICE SYSTEM?

CITIZEN INTERVENTION

Up until now, we have looked at the nature and extent of delinquency, its causes, and the different philosophies that underlie the juvenile just ce system. This chapter begins a look at how juveniles come in contact with the system and the procedures that affect their adjudication and disposition.

Figure 1 illustrates the first part of this process from its beginnings in the law up to the detention decision. The law, of course, reflects a legislative (and therefore societal) decision as to the types of behaviors necessary to draw an official response from the juvenile justice system. Obviously, violations of the criminal law are sufficient and constitute delinquent acts. In addition, the commission of status offenses also places a juvenile within the jurisdiction of the juvenile justice system. There is a third category of acts which might simply be called "deviant" acts that are not criminal. Spitting, cursing, and rudeness are examples of acts that are not normally illegal, but are deviant nonetheless (some states, however, have made acts like these criminal or status offenses). Once any of these deviant acts are included in the law, it becomes a crime or status offense and can be adjudicated by the juvenile justice system.

A law violation must, of course, be detected in order to be acted upon. As indicated in Chapter 2, the odds of being detected are not great. Several studies have been conducted that attempt to show the relationship between delinquent behavior and the possibility of being caught. One of the most interesting studies was conducted by Steffensmeier and Terry [1973]. They had people shoplift in a store while they knew they were being observed by actual shoppers in order to see if the shoppers would notify store employees. Interestingly, only 29 percent of the shoppers who saw the shoplifting notified store employees.

In a second part of their study, the investigators had the shoppers approached by a store official who asked them if they had seen an offense take place. The store official then pointed out the offender as a person under suspicion. Even given this strong prompting, 23 percent (of the total group) still refused to report the offender. As a result, observed cases of theft were reported only 29 percent of the time. Of course many more offenses occur than are ever

Figure 1. Juvenile Justice System - Part I   The Law through Juvenile Court Intake.

Legislative Decision to Criminalize	Law Violation	Detection of Violation	Police Decisions	Juvenile Court Intake Detention Decision

Criminal Law

Status Offense

Offense

Citizen, School, Parent, or Community Agency

Police

Street Diversion

Self-Report Studies [Undetected Crimes]

Juvenile Aid Bureau

Warn & Release

Refer to Counseling

Complaint Unfounded

Court Clerk [Complaint Filed]

Juvenile Court Intake

Detain Pending Hearing

Release Pending Hearing

All other 'deviant' acts

Out of System

Out of System

observed. Self-report studies provide an indication of how much more often delinquency occurs.

Besides the reports of observers, another way to gain entrance into the juvenile justice system is through the family. Parents or guardians can file a juvenile court petition against their children for status offenses or for delinquent behavior. It is not uncommon for a parent to refer a child to court who is ungovernable or habitually truant.

Many people have also claimed that there is a causal relationship between broken homes (one or no parent homes) and delinquency. The research investigating this connection has not been conclusive, however. Shaw and McKay looked at this relationship in Chicago during the 1930s. They compared the home situation of a sample of official delinquents with that of juveniles who had not been adjudicated delinquent. They found very little difference in the incidence of broken homes between these groups. Additional studies by Gold [1972], Hirschi [1969], and McCord, McCord, and Thurber [1962] have found no general relationship between parental absence and delinquency.

The point to keep in mind is that many children whose parents are not separated, widowed, or divorced suffer the same problems that some juveniles experience in broken homes. In a similar manner, many juveniles who live in single-parent homes receive the same support and attention as those juveniles in supportive two-parent homes. It appears likely that the quality of the parent-child relationship is more important than whether or not one or both parents is present. This assumption is supported by studies that have shown a link between delinquency and inconsistent discipline [Nye, 1938], marital discord [Smith and Walters, 1978], and parental criminality [Wilson, 1975].

Still another way parents can bring their children to the attention of the juvenile justice system is by victimizing them. No reliable data exist on the true extent of child abuse and neglect due to obvious reporting problems. However, at least two factors have been correlated with known cases: (1) Parents who suffered abuse as children tend to abuse their own children, and (2) Isolated and alienated families tend to become abusive.

In the first instance, it is felt that parents who were abused are unable to separate their childhood trauma from their relationship with their own children. Isolated families lack the support of friends and relatives who serve to relieve the pressures and stress of family relationships [Helfer and Kempe, 1968]. It is ironic that children have in the past been institutionalized for being victims of their own parents, but there is increasing reluctance in recent years (due to cases of neglect and maltreatment in state institutions) to institutionalize children in cases of parental neglect and abuse [See Murphy, 1975].

SCHOOLS & DELINQUENCY

While investigators differ in the degree to which schools play a role in delinquency, many of them feel it does play some part. This is only to be expected, considering the role played by schools in the life of juveniles. Beginning at age 4 or 5, juveniles spend most of their waking hours at school. In 1890, seven percent of the high school-aged population was in school. Today, 94 percent are in school. It is clear that school has become a primary method of socializing juveniles.

A number of studies have tested the link between school performance and delinquency. The 1967 President's Crime Commission reported that boys who failed in school were seven times more likely to become delinquent than those who did not fail. Subsequent investigations have confirmed this finding [Hirschi, 1969; Empey and Lubeck, 1971].

Travis Hirschi has found that failing grades alone do not cause delinquency, however. Based on his study of over 4,000 juveniles, he concluded that the causal chain is much more complex than this. Hirschi suggested that academic incompetence leads to poor school performance, resulting in dislike of school. This dislike results, further, in a rejection of the school's authority which ultimately results in delinquent behavior. His research found this linkage to hold true where low scores on achievement tests were linked to poor grades, which caused an attitude change toward school. He found this attitude change to cause juveniles to care less about teacher's opinions of them and led to delinquency.

Learning disabilities occur when there is a severe discrepancy between someone's expected achievement (based on scores of intelligence tests) and actual achievement, when the discrepancy is not attributable to mental retardation, physical handicap, or emotional disturbance. A number of investigators have examined the link between learning disabilities and delinquency where achievement is inhibited by a juvenile's problems with receiving, understanding, or communicating information.

A 1977 Senate Subcommittee on Delinquency described what they though to be the link between learning disabilities and delinquency.

> A learning disabled child has the mental capacity to master the material in school but is prevented from doing so by the disorder. Since the child appears to have the ability to succeed the failure may be mistakenly traced to laziness or lack of interest despite the fact that the child may be putting a great deal of effort into the work. The resulting frustration, humiliation and resentment can lead to emotional problems and ultimately behavioral difficulties... Thus the inability to successfully cope either on an academic or social level increases the chances of delinquency both in and out of school.

Despite this view, however, empirical research comparing juveniles with learning disabilities with other juveniles has been unable to establish a causal relationship between learning disabilities and delinquency. A review of the literature in this area was conducted in 1976 with the following result.

> As of the end of 1975, the existence of a causal relation between learning disabilities and delinquency has not been established; the evidence for a causal link is feeble. On the basis of the sketchy evidence so far produced, the notion that many delinquents have become so because of learning disabilities cannot be accepted. The notion that programs to diagnose and treat learning disabilities clearly will actually prevent delinquency is not supported by any data at all. Far from being "studied to death," as proponents of the LD/JD link sometimes claim the link has scarcely been studies at all. The existing work that meets normal minimal standards is fragmentary [Murray, 1976].

Other studies by McCullough et al. in 1979 and by Zimmerman and his associates in 1981 have had similar findings.

The available literature indicates that: (1) Self-report data shows that learning disabled juveniles commit no more delinquency than other youths, and (2) They are only slightly more likely to be adjudicated delinquent (rather than being released) when caught, compared to other juveniles. The reason why learning disabled youths are treated more severely by the juvenile justice system is probably due to their poor school performance or else their inability to present themselves in court as well as other children. Therefore, while learning disabilities do not cause delinquency, they do increase the likelihood of adjudication of juveniles whose delinquency is detected.

A third way that juveniles come in contact with the juvenile justice system in school situations is through violence and vandalism in schools, which has become an increasing concern in recent years. In New Jersey, for example, a mandatory reporting system was set up in 1979 whereby teachers are required to complete incident reports any time a criminal incident occurs in the school. These reports are sent to the State and are' compiled annually. Unfortunately, they have yet to produce reliable data due to reporting problems involving offense definitions, duplication, and underreporting.

Fortunately, in late 1979, two Columbia University researchers published the results of a nationwide survey they conducted of violence in the schools. Among their major findings is the fact that the vast majority of secondary schools do not have a serious problem with school crime. They found only eight percent of public schools in the United States to be seriously affected by crime, violence, and disruption. In a given month, for example, only about one-half of one percent (0.5%) of secondary school students or teachers have something taken from them by force, weapons, or threats [Ianni and Reuss-Ianni, 1979].

The authors concluded that while violence and disruption is very serious where it exists, it is not the widespread phenomenon we are sometimes led to believe.

> In a number of the schools we studied where there had been a decline in the incidence of school violence and vandalism, this decline had taken place during a period of time in which crime rates had soared in the immediate communities. In

some of these schools, parents reported that they
felt their children were safer when they were
within the school than they were in their own
communities... With minor exceptions, the risks
of being a victim of either attack or robbery in
schools decline steadily as grade level increases.

The authors also found that some common solutions to
school disruption were not solutions at all. They found
that temporary suspension causes students to fall further
behind in school, making them more prone to disruptive
behavior. They also observed that transferring
troublemakers to other schools merely shifts the location of
the problem. Finally, they found the leadership of the
principal to be important in that school spirit was more
effective than authoritarian school procedures in preventing
violence and vandalism.

THE POLICE ROLE IN DELINQUENCY

The role of police in juvenile justice is more varied and
flexible than it is in the adult justice system. Unlike the
adult system, police are expected to release offenders as
often as formally charge them in juvenile cases.

As might be expected, a subject that has drawn much
attention from investigators is, how do police exercise this
greater allowance for discretion? What factors influence
their custody or release decisions?

In 1964, Piliavin and Briar conducted the first empirical
investigation of police discretion in handling juveniles.
They observed all police-juvenile encounters in a West Coast
city over a nine-month period. It was found that police
generally have five alternatives in deciding how to handle a
suspected juvenile law violator: (1) Outright release, (2)
Release and submission of a "field interrogation report"
briefly describing the circumstances initiating the
encounter, (3) Official reprimand and release to parents or
guardian, (4) Citation to juvenile court, or (5) Arrest and
confinement in a detention facility.

Piliavin and Briar found that over 90 percent of all
police-juvenile encounters were for minor offenses, and
found the full range of alternatives was utilized by police
for almost every type of offense. However, if the crime was
serious enough, it was usually sufficient grounds for arrest
(even though 30 percent of the burglary cases and 12 percent

of the motor vehicle theft cases did not involve arrests). Perhaps their most interesting finding, however, was that the personal demeanor of the juvenile was usually more important than the type of offense in determining what action the police officer took. The more uncooperative the juvenile was with the police inquiry, the greater the likelihood that he or she was taken into custody. Once the juvenile was taken into custody, however, his or her prior record became the most important factor (at the police station).

In 1970, Black and Reiss observed police encounters with juveniles in Boston, Chicago, and Washington, D.C. They found that although black juveniles were taken into custody more often than white juveniles, this disparity was due to the complainant's preference in these cases. That is to say, 21 percent of blacks were arrested, while only eight percent of whites were arrested. However, 21 percent of black victims demanded that an arrest be made, whereas only 15 percent of the white victims demanded that the juvenile be arrested. When no complainant was present, police arrested whites 10 percent of the time and blacks 14 percent of the time. Therefore, racial differences can be largely attributed to citizen preferences, and not necessarily to police prejudices.

Black and Reiss also looked at the effect of demeanor on police decisions. Although the overwhelmingly majority (80 percent) of police-juvenile contacts were "civil" or "very deferential," as opposed to "antagonistic," they found no direct relationship between demeanor and arrest. As a result, Black and Reiss' observations in three cities found the most important factor in the police officer's decision to arrest was the complainant's preference that an arrest be made.

In 1978, Lundman, Sykes, and Clark replicated Black and Reiss' study in a large midwestern city. They discovered very similar results, finding no direct relationship between demeanor and arrest, but they found the complainant's preference to be important in police arrest decisions.

Looking back at Figure 1, it can be seen that once police take a juvenile into custody, they still have several options open to them in deciding how to handle a case. Most small police departments assign one officer the responsibility for handling juvenile matters for the entire department. When an officer on patrol encounters a juvenile crime suspect, he will often refer the case to the juvenile officer or, in larger departments, to a juvenile unit or division.

The National Advisory Commission Task Force on Juvenile Justice and Delinquency Prevention recommended in 1976 tha every police department with more than 75 sworn officers establish a separate juvenile unit or division. Today, nearly every department has either juvenile officers or a formal juvenile division. In recent years, there has been an effort to standardize the manner in which police handle juveniles to insure consistency in their discretionary decisionmaking. An example of a formal alternative to individual police discretion in these matters is the "juvenile aid bureau" (JAB), which is a unit within a police department responsible for handling juveniles. The JAB usually consists of the department's juvenile officers plus one or two counselors.

Juvenile aid bureaus are very common in New Jersey, for example, and a description of their functioning is provided by a 1979 evaluation of their operation. Three quarters of the juveniles referred to JABs are property offenders and most are first offenders. As Figure 1 illustrates, once a juvenile is referred to the JAB, several things can happen: warn and release, refer for counseling, or refer to juvenile court. In New Jersey, 37 percent of juveniles referred to JABs were warned and released, 17 percent were referred for counseling, and 46 percent were referred to juvenile court for adjudication. Even though a juvenile is handled by a JAB, therefore, there is nearly a 50 percent chance he or she still will be sent to juvenile court.

A closer examination of these figures reveals some problems, however, in the disposition of juvenile cases by juvenile aid bureaus. First, the proportion of juveniles being referred to court or counseling varied widely among jurisdictions indicating, perhaps, a need for standardized criteria to limit the possibility of discriminatory practices. Second, in only one percent of the nearly 500 cases examined did the counselor participate in the case disposition; so there was a failure to make use of the person whose expertise would make him or her the best able to determine which juveniles would benefit from counseling. Finally, the number of juveniles referred to other community agencies was small, and there was very little follow up contact with juveniles. As a result, it is impossible to determine how effective the counseling, release, or the juvenile court options were in preventing future delinquency.

Even where juvenile aid bureaus exist, however, police are not obligated to have all juvenile cases handled there. Police are usually able to handle juveniles based on their own discretion. Once again, police generally have five alternatives in deciding how to handle a juvenile: warn and release, refer to juvenile court, refer to a social welfare agency, refer to another police department (many times juveniles are sent back to the towns where they live if the offense is committed elsewhere), or refer to criminal court for prosecution as an adult.

Table 1. Police Disposition of Juveniles Taken into Custody

Year	Total	Release	Juvenile Court	Welfare Agency	Other PD	Crimina Court
1975	1,675,711	697,061	883,736	24,29	31,663	38,958
	100%	41.6	52.7	1.4	1.9	2.3
1977	1,782,049	679,230	948,677	53,165	31,562	69,415
	100	38.1	53.2	3.0	1.8	3.9
1979	1,594,306	552,039	913,934	25,034	26,184	77,185
	100	34.6	57.3	1.6	1.7	4.8
1981	1,383,380	468,212	802,734	20,796	21,025	70,013
	100	33.8	58.0	1.5	1.6	5.1
1982	1,141,122	371,432	671,771	18,443	17,679	61,797
	100	32.5	58.9	1.6	1.5	5.4

Source: Compiled from FBI Uniform Crime Reports.

Although there do not exist nationwide data regarding the handling of juveniles by JABs, national data exist indicating how police utilize these five alternatives once a juvenile is taken into custody. Table 1 indicates trends in the police disposition of juveniles for the last eight years. It can be seen, for instance, that in 1975 there were a total of 1,675,711 juveniles taken into custody by police nationwide. This number has decreased to nearly 1.1 million in 1982, reflecting the general decrease in the proportion of juveniles being arrested (as compared to adults) in recent years. In 1975, 41.6 percent of those juveniles taken into custody were handled within the department and released, while 52.7 percent were referred to juvenile court for adjudication. It can be seen, further, that the proportion of juveniles being sent to juvenile court has steadily increased to 58.9 percent in 1982, while the proportion released has steadily decreased over the years to 32.5 percent. There is no discernible trend in the proportion of juveniles referred to welfare agencies or other police departments, but there has been a steady increase in the proportion of juveniles referred to criminal court from 2.3 percent in 1975 to 5.4 percent in 1982.

It can be concluded from these data that the last eight years has witnessed a trend toward treating juveniles in a more serious manner. Increasing numbers of referrals to juvenile court and criminal court (now accounting for nearly two-thirds of all police dispositions of juveniles) indicate a greater willingness to adjudicate juveniles as delinquents or criminals. The next chapter will provide some reasons why we reached this point from the initial decision to treat juveniles as children in need of assistance over 80 years ago.

REFERENCES

Black, D.J. and Reiss, Albert J. Police Control of Juveniles. American Sociological Review, 35 [1970], 63-77.

Empey, LaMar T. and Lubeck, Steven G. Explaining Delinquency. Lexington, Ma.: Lexington Books, 1971.

Gold, Martin. Delinquent Behavior in an American City. Belmont, Ca.: Brooks/Cole, 1970.

Helfer, Ray and Kempe, C. Henry, Eds. The Battered Child. Chicago: University of Chicago Press, 1968.

Hirschi, Travis. Causes of Delinquency. Berkeley: University of California Press, 1969.

Ianni, Francis A.J. and Reuss-Ianni, Elizabeth. School Crime and the Social Order of the School. IRCD Bulletin, 14 [Winter, 1979], 206-214.

Lundman, Richard J., Sykes, Richard E., and Clark, John P. Police Control of Juveniles: A Replication. Journal of Research in Crime & Delinquency, 9 [1978], 235-246.

McCullough, B. Claire, Zaremba, Barbara A., and Rich, William D. The Role of the Juveniles Justice System in the Link Between Learning Disabilities and Delinquency. State Court Journal, 3 [1979], 45.

McCord, Joan, McCord, William, and Thurber, Emily. Some Effects of Paternal Absence on Male Children. Journal of Abnormal and Social Psychology, 64 [1962], 361-269.

Murphy, Patrick T. Our Kindly Parent... The State. New York: Penguin, 1975.

Murray, Charles A. The Link Between Learning Disabilities and Juvenile Delinquency: Current Theory and Knowledge. Washington, D.C.: U.S. Government Printing Office, 1976.

New Jersey State Law Enforcement Planning Agency. Juvenile Aid Bureaus. Trenton, N.J.: Evaluation Unit, 1979.

Nye, Ivan F. Family Relationships and Delinquent Behavior. New York: Wiley, 1938.

Piliavin, Irving and Briar, Scott. Police Encounters with Juveniles. American Journal of Sociology, 70 [September, 1964], 206-214.

President's Commission on Law Enforcement and Administration of Justice. Task Force Report: Juvenile Delinquency and Youth Crime. Washington, D.C.: U.S. Government Printing Office, 1967.

Smith, Richard and Walter, James. Delinquent and Non-Delinquent Males' Perceptions of Their Fathers. Adolescence, 13 [1978], 21.

Steffensmeier, Daryl J. and Terry, Robert M. Deviance and Respectability: An Observational Study of Reactions to Shoplifting. Social Forces, 51 [June, 1973], 417-426.

U.S. Senate Subcommittee on Delinquency. Challenge for the Third Century: Education in a Safe Environment. Washington, D.C.: U.S. Government Printing Office, 1977.

Wilson, Harriet. Juvenile Delinquency, Parental Criminality, and Social Handicap. British Journal of Criminology, 15 [1975], 241-250.

Zimmerman, J., Rich, W.D., Keilitz, I., and Broder, P.K.

Some Observations on the Link Between Learning Disabilities and Delinquency. <u>Journal of Criminal Justice</u>, 9 [1981], 1-17.

6. WHAT ARE THE LEGAL RIGHTS OF JUVENILES?

A SHORT HISTORY OF JUVENILE JUSTICE

It comes as no surprise that the way we deal with juveniles in criminal matters reflects the way we treat juveniles in other areas of life. The establishment of the first juvenile court in 1899 corresponded with the rise of positivism, which saw the environment as a cause of behavior. The 1800s also witnessed the establishment of houses of "Refuge" which were set up to protect wayward youths by reforming them in a family-like atmosphere. Such developments were a manifestation of the philosophy of parens patriae, giving the state the right of parental control over juveniles.

This "child-saving" movement led up to the establishment of the first juvenile court in Illinois, and marked a new era of jurisprudence. This juvenile court was a significant innovation in that the concept of justice was altered from adjudication of guilt to diagnosis of a condition. The emphasis of the justice process was changed from deterrence and incapacitation to rehabilitation, in order to assist and not to punish the juvenile. Behavior patterns were seen as being more important than specific acts because the acts were considered merely as symptoms of some underlying problem. Also, juvenile court proceedings were civil proceedings, rather than criminal proceedings, in order to serve best the interests of the child through informal adjudication involving no stigma of criminality [Mack, 1909].

By 1920, every state in the country had established a juvenile court based on these princ ples of positivism and the rehabilitative model. Although the idea of the juvenile court spread quickly, its implementation, however, was not carried out in a uni orm or standardized manner. As the President's Crime Commission pointed out in 1967,

> ...the mere passage of a juvenile court statute does not automatically establish a tribunal of the sort the reformers contemplated. A U.S. Children's Bureau survey in 1920 found that only 16 percent of all so-called juvenile courts in fact had separate hearings for children and an officially authorized probation service and recorded social information on children brought to court. A similar survey conducted... in 1966 revealed significant gaps still existing between

ideal and actual court structures, practices, and personnel. Indeed, it has been observed that "there is nothing uniform" in the operation of children's courts.

So although there was great consensus about how the juvenile court should operate, the implementation of this model was not consistent. This gap between the philosophy of the juvenile court and its actual functioning in practice ended in a court case early in the court's history.

Frank Fisher was a 14 year-old boy in Pennsylvania who was indicted for the crime of larceny. The prosecutor in the case felt that criminal prosecution was not required in the case, so Fisher was remanded by the judge to juvenile court where he was adjudicated delinquent and committed to a House of Refuge.

Fisher's case was appealed on the grounds that the Pennsylvania juvenile court (which was similar to that of most states) was unconstitutional. Among the challenges made was the fact that Fisher was denied the right to a trial by jury for his felony charge, and that the juvenile court allowed for different punishments for the same offense based on age. On these grounds, and others, the constitutionality of the existence of the juvenile court was challenged.

The Supreme Court of Pennsylvania heard this case in 1905 in Commonwealth v. Fisher. The court ruled, in part, that the legislature's establishment of the juvenile court was merely an exercise of the state's power to "save" children.

> ...the legislature, in directing how that duty
> is to be performed in a proper case, denies the
> child no right of a trial by jury, for the simple
> reason that by the act it is not to be tried for
> anything. The court passes upon nothing but the
> propriety of an effort to save it, and, if a
> worthy subject for salvation, that effort is made
> in the way directed by the act. The act is but an
> exercise by the state of its supreme power over
> the welfare of its children, a power under which
> it can take a child from its father and let it go
> where it will, without committing it to any
> guardianship or any institution, if the welfare of
> the child, taking age into consideration, can be
> thus best promoted.

Therefore, the Court held that the juvenile court is established for the salvation, and not punishment of children, and that no attempt at prosecution is being made--only an effort to look after the best interests of the child, as a parent would.

This decision was a precedent in this area and led the way for other state supreme courts in affirming the rehabilitative philosophy of the juvenile court. Such a commitment on the part of the judiciary to the founding philosophy of the juvenile court was continuously upheld until 1967. The rehabilitative model of juvenile justice was based, therefore, on the assumption that scientific knowledge about human behavior had reached the point where responsible predictions of the consequences of certain types of juvenile conduct could be made and effectively treated. The problem, unfortunately, was that such knowledge did not exist.

Despite the dominance of the rehabilitative juvenile court, based on the precepts of positivism, it always had its detractors. One of the leading critics of the philosophy of the juvenile court was Paul Tappan, who wrote during the 1940s. An excerpt from one of Tappan's articles, "Treatment without Trial," captures some of his objections to the rehabilitative model.

These various methods of applying court treatment without a full and fair judicial trial of the issue of guilt of a particular offense, despite their seductive rationale, appear to the writer to be particularly hazardous and unnecessary... For their greatest fault is in failing to give to the defendant some of the most basic protections of due process which inhere in our modern legal system. Under our constitutions and laws the defendant deserves at very least [1] a definite charge of a particular offense, [2] the right to be confronted by the witnesses from whom is derived the evidence on which he is convicted, [3] a [real] right to counsel and appeal, and [4] conviction only upon a preponderance of credible, competent, relevant evidence... The difficulties with this [current juvenile court] approach are basic: Where no specific and clear-cut offense categories are established most anyone can be adjudicated to a status carrying stigma and

potentially damaging treatment by correctional
agencies of criminal and quasi-criminal courts.
The utmost of discretion is left in the hands of
judicial and probation personnel unhampered by
statutory definitions or limitations, undirected
save by a very general principle of treating,
reforming, rehabilitating.

In addition to the lack of legal counsel and basic due
process protections, Tappan also charged that the juvenile
court must also measure up to the promise of scientific and
humane treatment.

Tappan's allegation of maltreatment of juveniles was not
far off the mark. Many state institutions set up to look
after the best interests of children, sometimes did not do
so. As Alexander Pisciotta has pointed out, abuses by the
state were occurring before the juvenile court was
established at the turn of the century.

...the available investigations and records of
nineteenth century juvenile institutions offer
compelling evidence that the state was not a
benevolent parent. In short, there was
significant disparity between the promise and
practice of parens patriae. Discipline was seldom
"parental" in nature, inmate workers were
exploited under the contract labor system,
religious instruction was often disguised
proselytization, and the indenture system
generally failed to provide inmates with a home in
the country. The frequency of escapes, assaults,
incendiary incidents, and homosexual relations
suggests that the children were not, as the
Pennsylvania court presumed in 1838, "separated
from the corrupting influence of improper
associates."

Examples of abuses like these added strength to Tappan's
claims that the "rehabilitative" juvenile court denied the
legal rights of juveniles in exchange for hypo hetical
benefits of dubious value.

Tappan's arguments received more and more support during
the 1950s, while support for the juvenile court's
rehabilitative model waned. Due to instances of abuses and
the failure of the state to reform children, greater
emphasis fell on issues such as legal fairness, the casual

use of detention, and the inability of the juvenile court to deliver on its promise to protect and reform juveniles. These criticisms ultimately led to changes in the juvenile court structure.

California and New York were the first states to reflect this changing outlook in their juvenile court statutes. California, for example, had a typical juvenile court system. Since its inception in 1915, a juvenile could be petitioned to court for any one of 14 violations including: begging, having no parental supervision, having no means of support, being abused or neglected, habitually visiting a poolroom or saloon, habitual truancy, refusal to obey parents, leading (or in danger of leading) an idle, dissolute, lewd or immoral life, being feeble-minded or insane, being afflicted with syphilis or gonorrhea, or violating the criminal law. Similar to other states, California's juvenile court provided no clear right to legal counsel, adjudication was based on a preponderance of the evidence (unlike "beyond a reasonable doubt" for adults), and the court's jurisdiction extended up to age 21.

In 1957, however, the governor of California appointed a commission to investigate the operation of the juvenile court in that state. Reporting in 1960, the commission confirmed many of Tappan's allegations.

> While supporting the fundamental protective and rehabilitative ideology of the socialized court, the Commission reported a number of serious deficiencies: [a] an absence of well-defined standards and norms to guide juvenile court work meant that dispositions were more often dependent upon the community where a child got into legal trouble than on the intrinsic merits of the case or the needs of the child; [b] basic legal rights of the child were neither uniformly nor adequately protected; [c] the quality of rehabilitative services was questionable and decisions about treatment plans often seemed based on consideration of expediency and administrative convenience rather than on consideration of the needs of the child; and [d] there was excessive and unwarranted detention of children [Brantingham, 1979:263].

The lack of due process protections afforded to juveniles sparked 31 recommendations from the commission, resulting in major modifications in the California juvenile court in 1961.

The juvenile court's jurisdiction was streamlined into three general categories: dependent, neglected, abused children; status offenses, and delinquency (criminal violations). Second, legal counsel became mandatory in serious (felony) cases. Third, a pre-trial diversion process was established (six months of "informal probation") to keep non-serious cases from being formally adjudicated. Fourth, a two-stage trial was established consisting of an adjudication (fact-finding) hearing and a disposition (sentencing) hearing, similar to the procedure for adults.

New York State followed California's lead in 1962, when it abolished its juvenile court and replaced it with a broader "Family Court." The revisions in New York were similar to those in California, but the due process emphasis was extended even further. For example, the New York State revisions expanded the use of legal counsel through the establishment of "law guardians," who were defense lawyers paid by the state to represent juveniles exclusively. This innovation rapidly escalated the role of defense counsel in juvenile court. By 1966-67, 96 percent of juveniles appearing in family court in New York City were represented by counsel.

So by 1962, the two largest states had systematically introduced legal counsel in juvenile court, restructured its jurisdiction, and changed its procedures from a focus on rehabilitation to a due process emphasis. It remained to be seen whether the rest of the country would embrace these changes.

THE 1960s: KENT & GAULT CASES

The emphasis on due process continued when the U.S. Supreme Court heard its first case involving the juvenile court in 1966. The Supreme Court summarized the case as follows:

> Morris A. Kent, Jr. first came under the authority of the Juvenile Court of the District of Columbia in 1959. He was then aged 14. He was apprehended as a result of several housebreakings and an attempted purse snatching. He was placed on probation, in the custody of his mother who had been separated from her husband since Kent was two

years old. Juvenile Court officials interviewed Kent from time to time during the probation period and accumulated a "Social Service" file.

On September 2, 1961, an intruder entered the apartment of a woman in the District of Columbia. He took her wallet. He raped her. The police found in the apartment latent fingerprints. They were developed and processed. They matched fingerprints of Morris Kent, taken when he was 14 years old and under the jurisdiction of the juvenile court. At about 3 p.m. on September 5, 1961, Kent was taken into custody by police. Kent was then 16 and therefore subject to the "exclusive jurisdiction" of the Juvenile Court... He was still on probation to that court as a result of the 1959 proceedings.

Upon being apprehended, Kent was taken to police headquarters where he was interrogated by police officers. It appears that he admitted his involvement in the offense which led to his apprehension and volunteered information as to similar offenses involving housebreaking, robbery, and rape. His interrogation proceeded from about 3 p.m. to 10 p.m. the same evening.

Some time after 10 p.m. petitioner [Kent] was taken to the Receiving Home for Children. The next morning he was released to the police for further interrogation at police headquarters, which lasted until 5 p.m.

The record does not show when his mother became aware that the boy was in custody but shortly after 2 p.m. on September 6, 1961, the day following petitioner's apprehension, she retained counsel.

Counsel, together with petitioner's mother, promptly conferred with the Social Service Director of the Juvenile Court. In a brief interview, they discussed the possibility that the Juvenile Court might waive jurisdiction...and remit Kent to trial by the District [criminal] Court. Counsel made known his intention to oppose the waiver.

Kent was detained at the Receiving Home for almost a week. There was no arraignment during this time, no determination by a judicial officer of probable cause for petitioner's apprehension...

Petitioner's counsel, in support of his motion

to the effect that the Juvenile Court should retain jurisdiction of petitioner, offered to prove that if Kent were given adequate treatment in a hospital under the aegis of the Juvenile Court [after a psychiatrist has certified that Kent "is a victim of severe psychopathology"], he would be a suitable subject for rehabilitation.

At the same time, Kent's counsel moved that the Juvenile Court should give him access to the Social Service file relating to Kent which had been accumulated by the staff of the Juvenile Court during Kent's probation period, and which would be available to the Juvenile Court judge in considering the question whether it should retain or waive jurisdiction. Kent's counsel represented that access to this file was essential to his providing Kent with effective assistance of counsel.

The Juvenile Court judge did not rule on these motions. He held no hearing. He did not confer with petitioner or petitioner's parents or petitioner's counsel. He entered an order reciting that after "full investigation, I do hereby waive" jurisdiction of the petitioner and directing that he be "held for trial for [the alleged] offenses under the regular procedure of the U.S. District Court for the District of Columbia." He made no findings. He did not recite any reason for the waiver. He made no reference to the motions filed by petitioner's counsel. We must assume that he denied sub silentio [without saying so], the motions for a hearing, the recommendation for hospitalization for psychiatric observation, the request for access to the Social Service file, and the offer to prove that Kent was a fit subject for rehabilitation under the Juvenile Court's jurisdiction.

Therefore, although Kent was only 16, the juvenile court judge had waived his jurisdiction and sent Kent to criminal court to be tried as an adult.

Kent subsequently was tried and convicted of burglary and robbery, but was found not guilty by reason of insanity on the rape charge. He was sentenced to 30-90 years in prison for the burglary and robbery.

His conviction was appealed on a number of grounds, all of

which involved alleged violations of due process. He contended that his initial interrogation and detention were unlawful because neither his parents, nor the juvenile court itself, were immediately notified of his arrest. Neither his parents or lawyer were present during the interrogation, and he was not informed of his right to an attorney as adults must be. Kent also alleged that he was deprived of his liberty (in detention) for about a week without a judicial determination of probable cause--another procedure required for adults. He also felt his fingerprints were taken in violation of the rehabilitative intent of the juvenile court.

Although the Supreme Court agreed that each of these "contentions raise problems of substantial concern," they restricted their decision to the judge's decision to waive Kent to criminal court. As Kent had alleged, the waiver was defective because no hearing was held, no reasons were given, no findings were made by the juvenile court, and his counsel was denied access to his social service file (which the judge presumably considered in his waiver decision).

The U.S. Supreme Court ruled in this case of Kent v. United States that the juvenile court should have "considerable latitude" to determine whether or not a juvenile's case should be waived to criminal court. They went on to say, however, that..

> It does not confer upon the Juvenile Court a license for arbitrary procedure. The statute does not permit the Juvenile Court to determine in isolation and without the participation or any representation of the child the "critically important" question whether a child will be deprived of the special protections and provisions of the Juvenile Court Act. It does not authorize the Juvenile Court, in total disregard of a motion for hearing filed by counsel, and without any hearing or statement of reasons, to decide--as in this case--that the child will be taken from the Receiving Home for Children and transferred to jail along with adults, and that he will be exposed to the possibility of a death sentence instead of treatment for a maximum, in Kent's case, of five years, until he is 21.
> We do not consider whether, on the merits, Kent should have been transferred; but there is no place in our system of law for reaching a result

of such tremendous consequences without ceremony--without hearing, without effective assistance of counsel, without a statement of reasons. It is inconceivable that a court of justice dealing with adults, with respect to a similar issue, would proceed in this manner. It would be extraordinary if society's special concern for children, as reflected in the District of Columbia's Juvenile Court Act, permitted this procedure. We hold that it does not.

It is clear that the Supreme Court did not agree with the manner in which the waiver decision was handled.

The net, therefore, is that petitioner--then a boy of 16--was by statute entitled to certain procedures and benefits as a consequence of his statutory right to the "exclusive" jurisdiction of the Juvenile Court. In these circumstances, considering particularly that decision as to waiver of jurisdiction and transfer of the matter to the District Court was potentially as important to Kent as the difference between five years confinement and a death sentence, we conclude that, as a condition to a valid waiver order, petitioner was entitled to a hearing, including access by his counsel to the social records and probation or similar reports which presumably are considered by the court, and to a statement of reasons for the Juvenile Court's decision. We believe that this result is required by the statute read in the context of constitutional principles relating to due process and the assistance of counsel.

As a result, all future waivers to criminal court must provide the juvenile with a hearing on the waiver, effective assistance of counsel, and a statement of reasons for the juvenile court's decision.

Later in its opinion, the Supreme Court went on to qualify the type of hearing required for a waiver.

We do not mean by this to indicate that the hearing held must conform with all of the requirements of a criminal trial or even of the usual administrative hearing; but we do hold that the hearing must measure up to the essentials of due process and fair treatment.

Therefore, the hearing is not to constitute a trial in itself, but it must be a fair and impartial hearing.

The Kent case is significant because it was the first time the U.S. Supreme Court examined juvenile court procedure, and it found that the procedure in question (waiver to criminal court) must measure up to the essentials of due process and fair treatment. Therefore, it can be seen that the due process trend begun in California and New York was continued at least for the narrow issue of waiver proceedings. As the Supreme Court suggested in its decision in the kent case, the failure of the rehabilitative model to live up to its promise and scientific and humane treatment was probably the largest factor in the changing emphasis toward due process.

> While there can be no doubt of the original laudable purpose of juvenile courts, studies and critiques in recent years raise serious questions as to whether actual performance measures match well enough against theoretical purpose to make tolerable the immunity of the process from the reach of constitutional guarantees applicable to adults. There is much evidence that some juvenile courts, including that of the District of Columbia, lack the personnel, facilities and techniques to perform adequately as representatives of the State in a parens patriae capacity, at least wit respect to children charged with law violation. There is evidence, in fact, that there may be grounds for concern that the child receives the worst of both worlds: that he gets neither the protections accorded to adults nor the solicitous care and regenerative treatment postulated for children.

It did not take long, however, for the U.S. Supreme Court to take its second case dealing with the juvenile court. It occurred the following year, and In re Gault became the most significant and far-reaching decision yet made regarding the juvenile court. The Court summarized the case as follows:

> On Monday, June 8, 1964, at about 10 a.m., Gerald Francis Gault and a friend, Ronald Lewis, were taken into custody by the Sheriff of Gila County. Gerald was then still subject to a six months' probation order which had been entered on

February 25, 1964, as a result of his having been in the company of another boy who had stolen a wallet from a lady's purse. The police action on June 8 was taken as the result of a verbal complaint by a neighbor of the boys, Mrs. Cook, about a telephone call made to her in which the caller or callers made lewd or indecent remarks. It will suffice for purposes of this opinion to say that the remarks or questions put to her were of the irritatingly offensive, adolescent, sex variety [author's note: the actual remarks made were in the form of three questions: "Do you give any?" "Are your cherries ripe today?" "Do you have big bombers?"].

At the time Gerald was picked up, his mother and father were both at work. No notice that Gerald was being taken into custody was left at the home. No other steps were taken to advise them that their son had, in effect, been arrested. Gerald was taken to the Children's Detention Home. When his mother arrived home at about 6 o'clock, Gerald was not there. Gerald's older brother was sent to look for him at the trailer home of the Lewis family. He apparently learned then that Gerald was in custody. He so informed his mother. The two of them went to the detention home. The deputy probation officer, Flagg, who was also superintendent of the Detention Home, told Mrs. Gault "why Jerry was here" and said that a hearing would be held in Juvenile Court at 3 o'clock the following day, June 9...

On June 9, Gerald, his mother, his older brother, and probation officers Flagg and Henderson appeared before the Juvenile Judge in chambers. Gerald's father was not there. he was at work out of the city. Mrs. Cook, the complainant, was not there. No one was sworn at this hearing. No transcript or recording was made. No memorandum or record of the substance of the proceedings was prepared. Our information about the proceedings and the subsequent hearing on June 15, derives entirely from the testimony of the Juvenile Court Judge, Mr. and Mrs. Gault and Officer Flagg at the habeas corpus proceeding conducted two months mater. From this, it appears that at the June 9 hearing Gerald was questioned by the judge about the telephone call. There was conflict as to what he said. His mother recalled

that Gerald said only that he dialed Mrs. Cook's
number and handed the telephone to his friend,
Ronald. Officer Flagg recalled that Gerald
admitted making the lewd remarks. Judge McGhee
testified that Gerald "admitted making one of
these [lewd] statements." At the conclusion of
the hearing, the judge said he would "think about
it." Gerald was taken back to the detention
home. He was not sent back to his own home with
his parents. On June 11 or 12, after having been
detained since June 8, Gerald was released and
driven home. There is no explanation in the
record as to why he was kept in the detention home
or why he was released.

The next day, the Gaults received an informal note from
Office Flagg that a further hearing on Gerald's delinquency
would be held on the morning of June 15.

   At the appointed time on Monday, June 15,
Gerald, his father and mother, Ronald Lewis and
his father, and Officers Flagg and Henderson were
present before Judge McGhee. Witnesses at the
habeas corpus proceeding differed in their
recollections of Gerald's testimony at the June 15
hearing. Mr. and Mrs. Gault recalled that Gerald
against testified that he had only dialed the
number and that the other boy had made the
remarks. Officer Flagg agreed that at this
hearing Gerald did not admit making the lewd
remarks. But Judge McGhee recalled that "there
was some admission again of some of the lewd
statements. He--he didn't admit any of the more
serious lewd statements." Again, the complainant,
Mrs. Cook, was not present. Mrs. Gault asked that
Mrs. Cook be present "so she could see which boy
had done the talking, the dirty talking over the
phone." The juvenile judge said "she didn't have
to be present at that hearing." The judge did not
speak to Mrs. Cook or communicate with her at any
time. Probation Officer Flagg had talked to her
once--over the telephone on June 9.
   At this June 15 hearing a "referral report" made
by the probation officers was filed with the
court, although not disclosed to Gerald or his
parents. This listed the charge as "Lewd Phone
Calls." At the conclusion of the hearing, the
judge committed Gerald as a juvenile delinquent to

the State Industrial School "for the period of his minority [that is, until age 21], unless sooner discharged by due process of law." An order to that effect was entered. It recites that "after full hearing and due deliberation the Court finds that said minor is a delinquent child, and that said minor is of the age of 15 years."

Because Gault was 15 years old and was sentenced to the juvenile institution until he was 21, he effectively received a sentence of six years. This interesting because the maximum penalty for an adult for this charge was two months in jail and a $50 fine.

Gault's case eventually reached the U.S. Supreme Court on seven separate grounds. Gault charged that the juvenile court procedure in Arizona was unconstitutional because of its failure to provide adequate notice of the charges against him, he was not advised of his right to counsel, his protection against self-incrimination was not observed, he was denied the right to confront and cross-examine witnesses against him, he had no right to appeal the juvenile court's holding in Arizona, no transcript was made of the proceedings, and the judge gave no reasons for his finding.

The U.S. Supreme Court examined each of these issues and their application in juvenile court. In the first instance, the Supreme Court agreed with Gault's contention that both a juvenile and his parents must be notified early and in writing of the charges against him. The Court reasoned in the following manner.

> The "initial hearing" in the present case was a hearing on the merits. Notice at that time is not timely; and even if there were a conceivable purpose served by the deferral proposed by the court below, it would have to yield to the requirements that the child and his parents or guardian be notified, in writing, of the specific charge of factual allegations to be considered at the hearing, and that such written notice be given at the earliest practicable time, and in any event sufficiently in advance of the hearing to permit preparation. Due process of law requires notice of the sort we have described--that is, notice which would be deemed constitutionally adequate in a civil or criminal proceeding. It does not allow a hearing to be held in which a youth's freedom

and his parent's right to his custody are at stake without giving them timely notice, in advance of the hearing, of the specific issues that they must meet.

The U.S. Supreme Court also used constitutional grounds to uphold Gault's claim that juveniles must be notified of their right to counsel, or to appointed counsel if they are indigent, where commitment to an institution can occur.

We conclude that the Due Process Clause of the Fourteenth Amendment requires that in respect of proceedings to determine delinquency which may result in commitment to an institution in which the juvenile's freedom is curtailed, the child and his parents must be notified of the child's right to be represented by counsel retained by them, or if they are unable to afford counsel, that counsel will be appoints to represent the child.

Because a delinquency proceeding is comparable to a serious felony prosecution, the Court supported the right to counsel in delinquency cases.

The Supreme Court also held that juveniles, like adults, should be afforded the protection against self-incrimination and the right to cross-examine witnesses against them.

We conclude that the constitutional privilege against self-incrimination is applicable in the case of juveniles as it is with respect to adults. We appreciate that special problems may arise with respect to waiver of the privilege by or on behalf of children, and that there may well be some differences in technique--but not in principle--depending upon the age of the child and the presence and competence of parents. The participation of counsel will, of course, assist the police, Juvenile Courts and appellate tribunals in administering the privilege. If counsel was not present for some permissible reason when an admission was obtained, the greatest care must be taken to assure that the admission was voluntary, in the sense not only that it was not the product of ignorance of rights or of adolescent fantasy, fright, or despair...
As we said in Kent v. United States with respect to waiver proceedings, "there is no place

in our system of law for reaching a result of such tremendous consequences without ceremony..." We now hold that, absent a valid confession, a determination of delinquency and an order of commitment to a state institution cannot be sustained in the absence of sworn testimony subjected to the opportunity for cross-examination in accordance with our law and constitutional requirements.

In order to prevent untrustworthy confessions and insure that sworn testimony is available, the Court ruled that there is no grounds for a distinction between adults and juveniles in these areas.

Nevertheless, the Supreme Court did not hold that juveniles had a right to appeal, to have transcripts of proceedings, or to a judge's reasons for his adjudication decision. The Court did address their desirability, however, in its ruling in Kent.

The Supreme Court's decision in Gault, therefore, made applicable to juveniles many of the due process protections that had been previously reserved for adults. Interestingly, Justice Stewart dissented from the Court's majority view in this case.

I believe that the Court's decision is wholly unsound as a matter of constitutional law, and sadly unwise as a matter of judicial policy.
Juvenile proceedings are not criminal trials. They are not civil trials. They are simply not adversary proceedings. Whether dealing with a delinquent child, neglected child, a defective child, or a dependent child, a juvenile proceeding's whole purpose and mission is the very opposite of the mission and purpose of a prosecution in criminal court. The object of one is the correction of a condition. The object of the other is conviction and punishment for a criminal act...
The inflexible restrictions that the Constitution so wisely made applicable to adversary criminal trials have no inevitable place in the proceedings of those public social agencies known as juvenile or family courts. And to impose the Court's long catalog of requirements upon juvenile proceedings in every area of the country

is to invite a long step backwards into the nineteenth century.

Justice Stewart's dissent expressed his belief that by the Supreme Court's ruling in Gault, it is completely turning its back on the rehabilitative model and is replacing it with an adult, criminal trial. Future Supreme Court decisions would confirm his fears.

THE 1970s: WINSHIP & McKEIVER

In order to find a person guilty of a crime in criminal court, historically, guilt must be proved beyond a reasonable doubt. From its inception, however, the juvenile court has been viewed as a civil proceeding. In civil cases, liability is determined by a preponderance of the evidence, which is a somewhat lower by a preponderance of the evidence, which is a somewhat lower burden of proof. It was this distinction that became the issue of the next major Supreme Court case regarding the juvenile court in 1970.

Winship was a 12 year-old boy from New York State who was taken into custody for entering a locker and taking $112 from a woman's pocketbook. In juvenile court, the judge acknowledged that the proof against Winship might not constitute proof beyond a reasonable doubt, but he denied Winship's contention that such proof was required by the 14th Amendment to the U.S. Constitution (which guarantees the due process protection of all citizens). The judge rejected this contention on the grounds that a preponderance of the evidence is all that is required in juvenile court, and a higher burden of proof is not necessary.

Winship was adjudicated delinquent and placed in a training school for boys for an initial period of 18 months, subject to annual extensions until he reached the age of majority at 18 years of age. Because he was 12 at the time, Winship effectively received a six-year sentence.

His appeal made it up to the U.S. Supreme Court on the grounds that his due process protections, as guaranteed by the 14th Amendment, had been violated. Therefore, the question before the Supreme Court was whether proof beyond a reasonable doubt was essential to the fair treatment of juveniles charged with an act that would be a crime if committed by an adult.

The Supreme Court agreed with Winship that such a burden

of proof is required.

> In sum, the constitutional safeguard of proof beyond a reasonable doubt is as much required during the adjudicatory stage of a delinquency proceeding as are those constitutional safeguards applied in Gault--notice of charges, the rights of confrontation and examination, and the privilege against self-incrimination. We hold, therefore, in agreement with Chief Judge Fuld in dissent in the Court of Appeals, "that, where a 12 year-old child is charged with an act of stealing which renders him liable to confinement for as long as six years, then, as a matter of due process... the case against him must be proved beyond a reasonable doubt."

As a result, proof beyond a reasonable doubt is now required during the adjudicatory stage of a delinquency proceeding.

The Court's rational in this case of In re Winship centered on the possibility of loss of liberty and the stigma of conviction for a juvenile.

> The accused during a criminal prosecution has at stake interest of immense importance, both because of the possibility that he may lose his liberty upon conviction and because of the certainty that he would be stigmatized by the conviction...
> Moreover, use of the reasonable-doubt standard is indispensable to command the respect and confidence of the community in application of the criminal law. It is critical that the moral force of the criminal law not be diluted by a standard of proof that leaves people in doubt whether innocent men are being condemned...
> In this context, I view the requirement of proof beyond a reasonable doubt in a criminal case as bottomed on a fundamental value determination of our society that it is far worse to convict an innocent man that to let a guilty man go free.

The higher burden of proof was also seen by the Court as necessary to maintain the confidence of the community as well as a "fundamental value" in America to avoid at all costs the conviction of an innocent man.

The Supreme Court's decision in the Winship case was not unanimous, however, and the dissent resulted from differing views regarding the philosophy and purpose of the juvenile court. Justice Harlan, for example, hoped the higher burden of proof would not obscure the rehabilitative ideals of the juvenile court.

> It is of great importance, in my view, that procedural strictures not be constitutionally imposed that jeopardize "the essential elements of the State's purpose" in creating juvenile courts. In this regard, I think it worth emphasizing that the requirement of proof beyond a reasonable doubt that a juvenile committed a criminal act before he is found to be delinquent does not [1] interfere with the worthy goal of rehabilitating the juvenile, [2] make any significant difference in the extent to which a youth is stigmatized as a "criminal" because he has been found to be a delinquent, or [3] burden the juvenile courts with a procedural requirement that will make juvenile adjudications significantly more time consuming, or rigid. Today's decision simply requires a juvenile court judge to be more confident in his belief that the youth did the act with which he has been charged.

On the other hand, Justices Burger and Stewart dissented on grounds that the rehabilitative model has, in effect, been negated in favor of treating juveniles as adult criminals.

> My hope is that today's decision will not spell the end of a generously conceived program of compassionate treatment intended to mitigate the rigors and trauma of exposing youthful offenders to a traditional criminal court; each step we take turns the clock back to the pre-juvenile-court era. I cannot regard it as a manifestation of progress to transform juvenile courts into criminal courts, which is what we are well on the way to accomplishing. We can only hope the legislative response will not reflect our own by having these courts abolished.

It is clear, in any case, that the due process model is almost fully in place with the Kent, Gault, and Winship decisions providing juveniles with many of the important constitutional protections already enjoyed by adults.

The Supreme Court continued its examination of the juvenile court in 1971 with the case, McKeiver v. Pennsylvania. Joseph McKeiver was 16 years-old and was in a group of 20-30 youths who pursued three other juveniles and took 25 cents from them. Following the Gault case, McKeiver had an attorney at his adjudication hearing, but he also asked for a jury trial and was denied it. He was adjudicated delinquent.

McKeiver's case was combined with three others by the U.S. Supreme Court to consider whether or not juveniles had the right to a trial by jury. According to the Sixth Amendment to the U.S. Constitution, "In all criminal prosecutions, the accused shall enjoy the right to a speedy and public trial, by an impartial jury of the state..." it was not clear, however, whether this would apply in juvenile court.

McKeiver argued that the Sixth Amendment is applicable to juveniles because juvenile court proceedings are "substantially similar to a criminal trial." He also claimed that juvenile detention an incarceration are substantially the same as jail and prison for adults. Furthermore, the procedures are the same and the stigma of delinquency is the same as an adult conviction. Finally, it was argued that a jury would not deny any of the supposed benefits of the juvenile justice process, such as wide discretion in sentencing.

The Supreme Court did not agree with this rationale and held that,

> Despite all these disappointments, all these failures, and all these shortcomings, we conclude that trial by jury in the juvenile court's adjudicatory stage is not a constitutional requirement.

Therefore, a trial by jury at the adjudicatory stage of a delinquency proceeding is not constitutionally required.

The Supreme Court's justification for its decision was based on several concerns. First, they did not feel that juries were a necessary part of a fair and equitable proceeding. Second, they were concerned with the possibility that juries would make juvenile proceedings into a fully adversary process. Third, juries would not add to the fact-finding function in juvenile court or remedy its defects. Furthermore, despite the grave disappointment of the juvenile court, "we are particularly reluctant to say... that the system cannot accomplish its rehabilitative goals."

Although the Supreme Court did not require juries in juvenile court, it did not prohibit them either.

> If, in its wisdom, any State feels that the jury trial is desirable in all cases, or in certain kinds, there appears to be no impediment to its installing a system embracing that feature. That, however, is the State's privilege and not its obligation.

Later in its opinion, the Court also gives freedom to individual juvenile court judges to experiment with juries.

> There is, of course, nothing to prevent a juvenile court judge, in a particular case where he feels the need, or when the need is demonstrated, from using an advisory jury.

Therefore, both the states and individual judges are free to make use of juries if they desire. The Supreme Court in this case merely said it is not making the use of juries a constitutional requirement in juvenile court. The Winship decision, therefore, apparently places a temporary stop to the growing trend toward providing juveniles with due process protections previously held only by adults.

LAWYERS IN JUVENILE COURT

It is important to recognize that Supreme Court decisions are not self-implementing. When the U.S. Supreme Court makes a decision, the states are the ones to put the new policy into practice. Sometimes, however, the effects of these new policies provide for unanticipated consequences.

Duffee and Siegel investigated the impact of one of the Supreme Court's most significant decisions--the Gault ruling that juveniles have the right to counsel at the adjudicatory stage of a delinquency proceeding. They were interested to see whether this new policy was having an effect on how juveniles were being treated in juvenile court. Other investigations had discovered, for example, that the presence of counsel resulted in more severe treatment of juveniles [Lemert, 1966].

A reason why such an inquiry is important is because investigations of the effect of other Supreme Court decisions have provided evidence that they are not always closely followed. For example, a study of the New York City Police Department following the Supreme Court decision in Mapp v. Ohio (which applied the exclusionary rule to the states, barring illegally seized evidence from trials), found that police were more likely to alter their court testimony than refrain from illegal searches [Kuh, 1962]. Similarly, investigations of the Miranda decision found that it had little effect on the way police conduct interrogations [Ayres, 1968; Reiss and Black, 1967].

It is usually not the case, of course, that criminal justice agencies simply ignore Supreme Court decisions. It is more often the case that the Supreme Court's ruling is twisted to conform with everyday demands of criminal justice agencies.

Duffee and Siegel wanted to see if this inefficient implementation of Supreme Court mandates would apply to the juvenile court as well. They believed that "when the appearance of due process has been maintained, the juvenile court should feel secure about future challenges and safer in prescribing even stricter control over its wards." As a result, they hypothesized that, "rates of incarceration and the presence of a lawyer are directly related. Or, in other words, juveniles without counsel are more likely to be released."

The authors looked at the effect the presence of a lawyer had on the likelihood that a juvenile would be sentenced to incarceration in a juvenile institution. They examined 218 cases handled in Albany County in New York State, and classified the seriousness of the offenses alleged into three levels: status offenses, minor crimes (misdemeanors), and major crimes (felonies).

Interestingly, they found that when the seriousness of the offense is held constant, the presence of counsel provides significantly more sentences to incarceration (and fewer dismissals). For both major and minor crimes, the likelihood of incarceration was 34 or 35 percent for juveniles represented by counsel, whereas no juveniles without counsel were incarcerated. As Duffee and Siegel concluded, "what does seem likely is that the juvenile court is more willing to retain a juvenile as a participant in the juvenile justice system when the presence of a lawyer has insured the appearance of due process." It appears, therefore, that the introduction of due process protections in juvenile court has had consequences beyond the intended goal of fair treatment.

REFERENCES

Ayres, Richard. Confessions and the Court. Yale Alumni Magazine, [December, 1968].

Brantingham, Paul J. Juvenile Justice Reform in California and New York in the Early 1960's. In F.L. Faust and P.J. Brantingham, Eds. Juvenile Justice Philosophy. [Second Edition]. St. Paul, Minn.: West Publishing, 1979.

Duffee, David and Siegel, Larry. The Organization Man: Legal Counsel in the Juvenile Court. Criminal Law Bulletin, 7 [1971], 544.

Kuh, L. The Mapp Case One Year After: An Appraisal of Its Impact in New York. New York Law Journal, [September 19, 1962].

Lemert, Edwin. Social Action and Legal Defense. Chicago: Aldine, 1966.

Mack, Julian W. The Juvenile Court. Harvard Law Review, 23 [1909], 104.

Pisciotta, Alexander W. Saving the Children: The Promise and Practice of Parens Patriae, 1838-98. Crime & Delinquency, 28 [July, 1982], 410-425.

President's Commission on Law Enforcement and Administration of Justice. Task Force Report: Juvenile Delinquency and Youth Crime. Washington, D.C.: U.S. Government Printing Office, 1967.

Reiss, Albert J. and Black, D.J. Interrogation and the Criminal Process. Annals. 374 [1967], 47.

Tappan, Paul W. Treatment without Trial. Social Forces, 24 [1946], 306.

7. WHAT ARE THE PROCEDURES OF JUVENILE COURT ?

ALTERNATIVES IN ADJUDICATION

The juvenile justice system is a bit more complicated than the adult justice system in that a juvenile can be dealt with in many more ways than can adults. As you recall, the diagram of the juvenile justice system began in Chapter 5 from a law violation to the police to detention pending a court appearance. The second half of the juvenile process is diagrammed in Figure 1, and follows the process from juvenile court intake to the ultimate disposition of a case.

At intake, a juvenile court judge or a probation officer makes an initial decision on how to handle a particular case. This screening decision can usually result in one of five outcomes. First, a juvenile may be transferred to another court. A determination of jurisdiction is based on whether the juvenile is under the age of majority or whether a hearing will be held for a waiver to criminal court.

A second route that may be decided upon at intake is to refer the juvenile to an intake or pre-judicial conference. many juvenile courts have a probation officer who will meet with the juvenile at the intake conference to discuss the charge. If the charge is not serious and the juvenile admits to committing the offense, the case can be closed without further action. As Figure 1 indicates, the case may be continued pending fulfillment of conditions such as restitution, psychological counseling, or social assistance. If these options are not appropriate, the case can be closed with only a recommendation made for referral to a social welfare agency, or the case may be held inactively with no official action being taken, as long as the juvenile stays out of further legal trouble for a certain period of time. If the juvenile denys the charge, or fails to appear at the intake conference, however, there is an automatic referral to juvenile court for adjudication.

A third alternative at the screening stage is the referral of a case to a juvenile conference committee. The juvenile conference committee (JCC) is a group of citizens appointed by the juvenile court to recommend a disposition for the juvenile in non-serious cases. Where they exist, the JCC is comprised of residents of the town where the juvenile lives in order to involve the community in the justice process. Normally, only first and minor offenders are referred to the

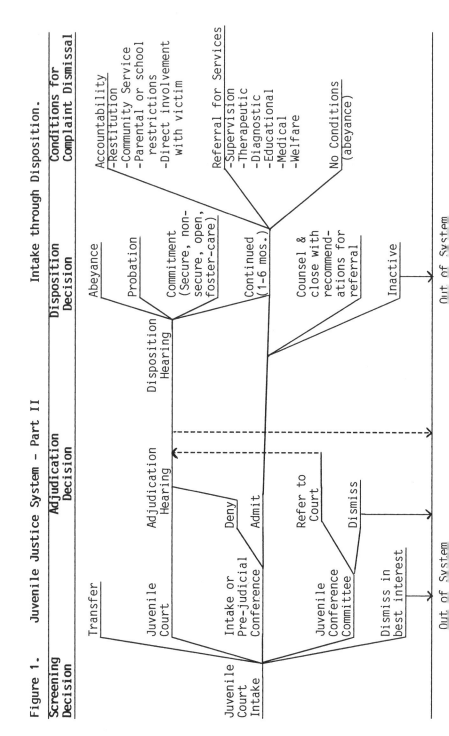

Figure 1. Juvenile Justice System - Part II   Intake through Disposition.

juvenile conference committee.

Once a juvenile is referred to the JCC, there are generally two alternatives. If the juvenile denies the charge, he or she must be sent to juvenile court for adjudication. As Figure 1 illustrates, the JCC can also dismiss the case while making recommendations for counseling, tutoring, or restitution.

A fourth alternative at the intake conference is dismissal of the case without further action. This occurs in minor cases that do not appear to require action by the juvenile court. A 15 year-old first offender who is referred to court for having beer on his breath might be an example of such a case. In these instances, it is clear that there are better things for the justice system to do.

The last alternative is, of course, juvenile court. The adjudicatory stage of juvenile court is the equivalent of an adult trial. This is a hearing on the petition against the juvenile where the facts of the case are established. Since the Gault decision in 1967, all juveniles charged with delinquency have the right to an attorney at this stage. Of course, if it is shown that the juvenile did not commit the acts alleged, the petition will be dismissed (as indicated by the dotted line in Figure 1). If it is found that the juvenile committed the delinquent act, he or she will be adjudicated either a delinquent or a status offender (depending on the precise behavior alleged).

Once a juvenile is adjudicated delinquent or a status offender, the juvenile court judge usually adjourns the case and sets a date for a disposition hearing. In the meantime, a probation officer completes a background investigation of the juvenile to help the judge in deciding on a disposition.

The disposition hearing in juvenile court is analogous to a sentencing hearing in criminal court. It is here that the judge determines the best way to resolve the case. As Figure 1 illustrates, the juvenile court judge has a number of options in choosing a disposition. He can hold the case in abeyance for six, nine, or 12 months, which usually means "continuance in contemplation of dismissal." If the juvenile does not get into further legal trouble within a designated period, the case can be dismissed without further action. This leaves the judge an opportunity to re-sentence the juvenile if he or she continues to have problems obeying the law.

A juvenile court judge can also choose to place a juvenile on probation. Probation involves having the offender serve the sentence in the community under the supervision of the court. The juvenile normally would be supervised by a probation officer on a weekly or monthly basis for one, two, or three years, similar to the adult system.

The third option for a disposition is a commitment to a juvenile facility or institution. Juveniles involved in serious delinquent behavior may be committed to a secure facility, which would be analogous to an adult prison. Non-secure facilities would include training schools and camps for delinquent children. Community-based programs include youth development centers, foster-care, and independent living arrangements.

The last dispositional alternative would be to continue the case pending fulfillment of certain conditions. In these cases, the juvenile would be obligated to undergo diagnostic or therapeutic services, or else make restitution to the victim, observe a curfew, or perform a community service. The completion of these obligations would have to take place within a certain period of time (usually one to six months) in order for the case to be terminated. Otherwise, the judge may re-sentence the juvenile if the conditions are not met.

FACTORS IN JUVENILE DISPOSITIONS

As Figure 1 illustrates, juvenile court judges have a great deal of discretion in deciding upon an appropriate disposition for a juvenile. From outright dismissal to commitment to an institution, a juvenile may be sentenced in any number of ways that can involve many different conditions. This large amount of "running room" has caused concern among some observers that juveniles may be treated inconsistently or arbitrarily.

In his book, The Child Savers, Anthony Platt examines the history of the juvenile court and claims that the "child savers" who founded it were not necessarily interested in the best interests of the child.

> They promoted correctional programs requiring
> longer terms of imprisonment, long hours of labor
> and militaristic discipline, and the inculcation

of middle-class values and lower-class skills...

The child-saving movement had its most direct consequences on the children of the urban poor. The fact that "troublesome" adolescents were depicted as "sick" or "pathological," were imprisoned "for their own good," and were addressed in a paternalistic vocabulary, and exempted from criminal law processes, did not alter the subjective experiences of control, restraint, and punishment.

As a result, Platt believes that juveniles of certain backgrounds (i.e., minorities and the poor) received more severe dispositions in juvenile court, not because of the crimes they committed, but because they had been stereotyped or discriminated against either consciously or unconsciously by juvenile court officials. Furthermore, Platt feels that this discrimination continues today.

The "invention" of delinquency consolidated the inferior social status and dependency of lower-class youth.

The child-saving ethic still motivates contemporary programs of delinquency control, though its application is far more tough-minded and unsentimental than it was sixty years ago [1977:176-8].

Edwin Schur concurred with Platt's view in his book, <u>Radical Non-Intervention</u>. He also believed that certain disadvantaged groups in society were being adjudicated more severely in juvenile court than were others who committed the same offenses.

The philosophy of the juvenile court--with its thorough-going social investigation of the alleged delinquent, and its relative lack of concern with the particular offense--virtually ensures that stereotypes will influence judicial dispositions. Sending the child who comes from a "broken home" in the slums to a training school, while giving probation to a youngster from a "good family" may not strike the judge as an exercise in stereotyping. He will consider them to be in the best interests of all concerned. As we have seen, however, such stereotypes tend to be self-confirming. Children from "broken homes" are likely to be committed to institutions because they are believed to be delinquency-prone; yet these very commitments, in turn, serve to reinforce that belief [1973:121].

Schur believes, therefore, that once a judge institutionalizes a juvenile because he comes from a broken home [when he would not have committed him if he had a family that was intact], the juvenile becomes an official delinquent with a record of incarceration simply because he comes from a one-parent home. This record will, in turn, increase the odds that he will be institutionalized again in the future.

Neither Schur or Platt present convincing data to support their claims, however. It has only been during the last 10 years that rigorous empirical investigations have taken place to determine whether or not these claims are true, and whether reform is needed in the handling of juvenile dispositions.

Perhaps the most comprehensive investigation of the factors that influence juvenile dispostions was conducted by Lawrence Cohen in 1975. He examined all juvenile court decisions in three counties during the course of an entire year. Denver County, Memphis-Shelby County, and Montgomery County (Pa.) were all included due to their mixture of age, sex, race, and income levels, and because of the comprehensive data collected in those juvenile courts.

Cohen gathered information on nearly 13,000 juveniles who appeared in juvenile court in these counties, and he examined the effect of their age, sex, ethnicity, socioeconomic status, family situation (broken homes), whether the juvenile was working, attending school, or idle, the number of prior court referrals, seriousness of the offense (as assessed by local officials), whether the court referral was made by police or others, whether the juvenile was in detention pending his court appearance, and whether there was a formal petition against the juvenile (or informal handling) in the case. The severity of the disposition was gauged from the least severe to the most severe (i.e., unofficially adjusted, case continued, formal probation, or incarceration).

Interestingly, Cohen did not find age, sex, race, broken homes, socioeconomic status or the seriousness of the offense to be significantly related to the seriousness of the disposition.

It seems, then, that for each court, the variable explaining the greatest amount of variation in the severity of the accorded disposition is a prior processing decision. In Denver and Memphis-Shelby Counties it is the decision to file a formal petition [rather than handle the case informally] that is most substantially and independently related to the criterion; in Montgomery County [where all cases are handled by a formal petition] it is the decision to detain the child that appears to independently influence the final disposition of the child's case [1975:44].

Therefore, the initial decision to handle the case in a serious manner (through a formal petition or through the use of pre-trial detention) affects the severity of the disposition more than any other factor.

These, somewhat surprising, findings led Cohen to examine the factors that explain these initial decisions. That is, if prior processing decisions are important to the ultimate disposition, what factors influence these prior processing decisions?

The most important factors in this analysis varied among the courts. In Denver, the most important factor was the seriousness of the offense, followed by prior court referrals and whether the juvenile was in detention prior to his hearing. In Memphis, the seriousness of the offense was most influential, followed by whether the case was referred by police and whether the juvenile was in detention. In Montgomery County, however, the most significant factor was whether the juvenile was idle, whether an agency other than the police referred the case to court, and whether the juvenile was from a broken home. Because these factors vary considerably among the courts, no general conclusions can be drawn. However, it is clear that the source of the referral to court, whether the juvenile came from a broken home, and whether or not the juvenile was detained should not, in themselves, be factors in the disposition decision. On the other hand, the fears of Platt were not realized in this investigation because race or social class were not significant factors in any county studied and, therefore, no evidence of discrimination based on these factors was found.

There is room for concern, nevertheless, when one realizes how poorly the significant factors account for the dispositions. Generally, the most important factors in each county accounted for only about 14 percent of the decisions made. That is to say, given complete information on each of the most significant factors for each county, you could only expect to predict accurately the disposition in the case 14 percent of the time. As Cohen concluded,

> although the factors most closely associated with these prior treatment decisions appear to vary considerably among the three courts, our ability to account for a large proportion of the variance in these decisions is limited. This inability to predict important decision outcomes, as well as the finding that prior processing decisions are closely related to subsequent decisions, raises a number of interesting questions [1975:51].

Some of the questions that remain would include: Are there unexamined factors that are actually accounting for these dispositions (e.g., complainant's preference)? Is it possible to adequately capture the reasons for a judge's decisionmaking from the written record (e.g., demeanor of the juvenile a factor)? Just because there was no apparent discrimination on the basis of race or socioeconomic status in these counties, is it not possible for it to exist elsewhere? As a result, investigations in other courts would be necessary in order to rule out the possibility of arbitrary dispositions in juvenile court.

It is interesting that in the three counties studied by Cohen, only a juvenile's detention pending adjudication was a significant factor in all three counties. Explanation of the detention decision had been the focus of several investigations which, unlike the studies of court dispositions, have had somewhat more consistent results.

Helen Sumner examined the factors in the detention decision of 10 California counties, Richard Chused investigated detention decisions in three New Jersey counties, and Lawrence Cohen re-examined Denver, Memphis-Shelby, and Montgomery Counties with regard to their detention practices. It is interesting that the use of detention varies considerably among jurisdictions. Some counties detain only 19 percent of the juveniles referred to court, while others place up to 80 percent in detention.

Presumably, these wide variations could be expected to reflect differences in the seriousness of crimes committed by juveniles in these areas. In a county with many serious juvenile offenses, for example, you might expect a higher rate of detention. Unfortunately, this is not the case.

In no county investigated by Sumner, Chused, or Cohen was the seriousness of the offense found to be a significant factor. Furthermore, age, race, and sex generally appear to play little or no role in the detention decision.

As it turns out, the juvenile's prior record was the most consistent factor in the detention decision; the more serious the prior record, the more likely it was that he or she would be placed in detention pending adjudication. There was also evidence in each of the three studies that juveniles from broken homes and those who were not working or in school were more likely to be detained. This finding is significant inasmuch as neither idleness or family status are appropriate factors for consideration in the detention decision. It is important to keep in mind Schur's warning that unconscious stereotypes may underlie important court decisions and create, rather than eliminate, problems of delinquency. Future investigations should carefully examine the basis for the disposition and detention decisions, because these decisions can be turning points in the lives of juveniles. As a result, they should be based solely on legally-relevant criteria, without penalizing a juvenile for being the victim of a social situation that he or she cannot control.

DOUBLE JEOPARDY?

In 1971, a juvenile court petition was filed against a 17 year-old boy in Los Angeles, California. The petition alleged the juvenile had committed an armed robbery. There was a detention hearing and the juvenile was placed in detention pending adjudication.

At the adjudication hearing, the court took testimony from two witnesses and from the juvenile. The judge found that the allegation of armed robbery to be supported by the evidence, and he adjudicated the juvenile delinquent. The judge then ordered the youth detained pending a disposition hearing.

At the disposition hearing, the judge said that he finds the juvenile "not amenable to the care, treatment and training program available through the facilities of the juvenile court." The juvenile's defense counsel immediately asked for a continuance "on the ground of surprise." The disposition hearing was re-scheduled for the following week.

After a week passed, the judge, after considering the report of the probation officer, declared the juvenile "unfit for treatment as a juvenile," and ordered that he be prosecuted as an adult. The juvenile was subsequently tried and convicted in criminal court of armed robbery, and he was committed to the California Youth Authority.

The case eventually drew the attention of the U.S. Supreme Court when it was alleged that the juvenile's Fifth Amendment protections were violated. The Fifth Amendment to the U.S. Constitution reads, in part,

> ...nor shall any person be subject for the same offense to be twice put in jeopardy of life and limb.

This means that a person cannot be criminally prosecuted twice for the same offense. This commonly known as protection against double jeopardy.

The Supreme Court explained why such a protection is included in the Constitution.

> Because of its purpose and potential consequences, and the nature and resources of the State, such a proceeding imposes heavy pressures and burdens--psychological, physical, and financial--on the person charged. The purpose of the Double Jeopardy Clause is to require that he be subject to the experience only once "for the same offense."

The case was eventually decided in 1975 in Breed v. Jones.

The Supreme Court considered two main arguments in this case espousing the view that the procedure did not constitute double jeopardy. The first argued that double jeopardy was not violated because the procedure in the case was analogous to those cases permitting re-trial after reversal of a conviction on appeal. The Supreme Court did not agree with this view.

The Court has granted the Government the right to retry a defendant after a mistrial only where 'there is a manifest necessity for the act, or the ends of public justice would otherwise be defeated.'

Respondent was subjected to the burden of two trials for the same offense; he was twice put to the task of marshaling his resources against those of the State, twice subjected to the "heavy personal strain" which such an experience represents.

A second argument was advanced holding that consideration of this as double jeopardy would diminish the flexibility and informality of juvenile court proceedings without conferring any additional due process benefits. The Supreme Court rejected this view as well.

Transfer provisions represent an attempt to impart to the juvenile-court system the flexibility needed to deal with youthful offenders who cannot benefit from the specialized guidance and treatment contemplated by the system.

We do not agree with petitioner that giving respondent [juvenile] the constitutional protection against multiple trials in this context will diminish the flexibility and informality to the extent those qualities relate uniquely to goals of the juvenile-court system.

The Supreme Court's final ruling in this case held that adequate constitutional protections for the juvenile were lacking.

We hold that the prosecution of respondent in [criminal] court, after an adjudicatory proceeding in Juvenile Court, violated the Double Jeopardy Clause of the Fifth Amendment, as applied to the States through the Fourteenth Amendment.

As a result, the Breed v. Jones decision by the Supreme Court continues the trend in applying due process protections in juvenile court proceedings. As begun in Kent, Gault, and Winship, the distinction between juvenile and adult proceedings appears to be rapidly diminishing.

REFERENCES

Chused, Richard. The Juvenile Court Process: A Study of Three New Jersey Counties. Rutgers Law Review, 26 [Winter, 1973], 488-589.

Cohen, Lawrence E. Delinquency Dispositions: An Empirical Analysis of Processing Decisions in Three Juvenile Courts. Washington, D.C.: U.S. Government Printing Office, 1975.

Cohen, Lawrence E. Pre-Adjudicatory Detention in Three Juvenile Courts. Washington, D.C.: U.S. Government Printing Office, 1975.

Platt, Anthony M. The Child Savers: The Invention of Delinquency. [Second Edition]. Chicago: University of Chicago Press, 1977.

Schur, Edwin. Radical Non-Intervention: Rethinking the Delinquency Problem. Englewood Cliffs, N.J.: Prentice-Hall, 1973.

Sumner, Helen. Locking Them Up. Crime & Delinquency, 17 [April, 1971], 168-179.

8. CAN WE PREVENT JUVENILE DELINQUENCY ?

PRIMARY v. SECONDARY PREVENTION

Perhaps the oldest question in juvenile justice is, what
is the best way to deal with juveniles who break the law? A
common road-block in this inquiry is how we choose to
measure success.   That is, when would you consider your
delinquency prevention program a success?

Most often, recidivism (the commission of a new offense)
is regarded as the criterion for success. Unfortunately,
such a measure ignores an important characteristic of
delinquent behavior. That is, as self-reports have shown,
nearly all juveniles commit delinquent acts. Therefore, to
expect a delinquency prevention program to prevent all
delinquency is not being realistic.

The solution to this dilemma, nevertheless, can also be
found in the findings of self-report studies. Self-reports
tell us that, although many juveniles commit crimes, few do
so frequently and few commit serious offenses. Perhaps it
is most appropriate, therefore, to expect a delinquency
program to prevent the development of serious and frequent
offenders.

Once we agree on our measure of success, however, the
difficult part still remains. That is, how do you design a
delinquency prevention program that prevents the commission
of serious offenses? The answer lies in causation. When
you go to the doctor for hives, it is unlikely he will
prescribe a lotion for the irritation and tell you to go
home. He will probably attempt to determine why you have
hives and treat the cause, whether it be an allergy, a rare
disease, or poison ivy.   Likewise, delinquency prevention
strategies should be based on the causes of delinquency.

The question of when your prevention strategy should be
employed requires two answers.   Primary prevention
strategies attempt to prevent delinquency before it becomes
frequent or serious. Secondary prevention strategies
attempt to prevent the repetition of frequent or serious
delinquency.   As a result, two different types of
delinquency prevention strategies may be needed: one to
intervene in the delinquent careers of serious or frequent
offenders, and another aimed at changing the conditions that
lead to serious delinquency.

Before we look at some actual prevention efforts, there is

-98-

one additional point to recognize. When you go to the doctor, he does not prescribe the same medication each time. Likewise, an attorney does not claim the same defense in every case. Obviously, there are different causes for various illnesses, just as there are different defenses that are applicable in certain situations. In a similar manner, people behave in different ways for various reasons. Therefore, it is unlikely a single prevention strategy will work for everybody, because people commit crimes for different reasons. Although this appears to be a straightforward conclusion, people are continually seduced by crime prevention strategies advertised as "cure-alls." James Finckenauer has called this the "panacea phenomenon," to indicate that it simply does not make sense to expect any single type of program to effectively reduce delinquency. To expect this, would be analogous to expecting aspirin to cure all disease or the entrapment defense to be pertinent in all trials.

As a result, the most important issues of delinquency prevention are three: (1) Prevention strategies should be based on the causes of delinquency, (2) Primary and secondary prevention may require different types of strategies, and (3) People commit crimes for different reasons so it is unlikely that a single prevention strategy will work for everybody. Although these issues are not profound, it is surprising that relatively few delinquency prevention efforts explicitly recognize their importance.

If you were a supporter of Lombroso's explanation of criminality, for instance, and believed that criminals were biological throwbacks on the evolutionary scale, your proposals for delinquency prevention would undoubtedly be drastic. In order to base your program on the causes you identify, only proposals such as sterilization or preventive detention of atavists would likely be effective. Clearly, if you see crime as an inherited trait, the consequences for prevention would be severe.

In a similar way, supporters of Sheldon's notion of body-type as an important factor in delinquency would result in equally frightening consequences. Only through preventive detention or selective breeding to eliminate mesomorphs would the cause of delinquency be removed. Fortunately, neither Lombroso's or Sheldon's explanations of delinquency have been found to be correct.

One of the best known attempts at delinquency prevention

was the Cambridge-Somerville Youth Study conducted in Massachusetts beginning in 1935. The program was based on the assumption that psychological factors were a primary cause of delinquency. The investigators began by putting together a list of nearly 2,000 boys under 12 years of age gathered from teachers, probation officers, the police, and other agencies. They selected 650 boys from this list, some of whom had been identified as "pre-delinquents," and some who had not been so identified. Background information was collected for each boy on school performance, psychological tests, parental information, and social agency data.

The group of 650 boys was split in two groups of 325 each which were matched on nearly 100 factors, including age, religion, intelligence, personality, school performance, neighborhood, and many other factors. Because each boy had a matched counterpart in the other group, it was felt that the amount of delinquency in the groups should be about the same.

In order to see if they could prevent delinquency, they provided one group with counseling (psychotherapy) and with social services and assistance, but provided the other group with no services at all. They continued the experiment for 10 years. The results are summarized in Table 1.

Table 1. Cambridge-Somerville Youth Study Results.

	Boys Committing Any Offenses	Boys Committing Serious Offenses
Treatment Group (325 boys)	90 (28%)	76 (23%)
Control Group (325 boys)	85 (26%)	67 (21%)

Source: Powers and Witmer, 1951.

As Table 1 indicates, the treatment group who received the counseling committed slightly more crimes and more serious crimes than did the control group. It does not appear, therefore, that the counseling services were useful in preventing delinquency.

It should not be surprising, however, that even a large scale experiment like the Cambridge-Somerville Youth Study was not successful in preventing delinquency. Certainly an important reason why it failed is because it violated all three principles important to prevention programs. First, the treatment was not based on any theory of causation. As Finckenauer has recognized,

> The study had a stated hypothesis, that delinquent and potentially delinquent boys could be diverted from criminal careers if they were given continued friendship by adults who were interested in them and who could help them to obtain needed community services. However, the only basis for this hypothesis seems to have been Dr. Cabot's opinion, actually more of a hunch, based upon his own experience [1982:15].

Second, there was no distinction made between primary and secondary prevention.

> He [Cabot] seemed to be assuming that the disorder in question was like a medical disorder, in that it transcended the differences in the subjects in which it appeared, and that the treatment method to be employed was also sufficiently uniform that variation in its application from case to case could be disregarded... To give a great variety of services to a great variety of boys, each practitioner doing what he thinks best without reference to any commonly held body of theory, seems... no more a scientific experiment than a medical one would be in which different kinds of medicine were given to patients suffering from different kinds of disorders by doctors who held different theories as to the causes of the illnesses [Powers and Witmer, 1951].

Third, it is simply not realistic to expect a single type of prevention strategy to work for everybody.

> ...the chief lesson of this experiment is that there is no one answer, no one form of service by which all manner of boys can be helped to deal with the difficulties that stand in the way of their healthy incorporation of social norms, which is the essence of good social adjustment.

The failure of this experiment to reduce delinquency, therefore, should not be a surprise. This is not to say that counseling is necessarily useless. It merely indicates that one type of treatment cannot be expected to correct everyone's problems.

Perhaps the most ambitious delinquency prevention program ever attempted was Mobilization for Youth. It was directed at an entire neighborhood on the lower east side of Manhattan comprising over 20,000 people. The program began with a three-year grant of $12.5 million and ultimately received over $30 million in grants from the government and from private foundations between 1962 and 1968.

The goal of Mobilization for Youth (MFY) was to reduce delinquency by improving the conditions of life through expanding opportunities for legitimate success. Clearly, the assumption was that delinquency emanates from sociological, rather than psychological, influences; because the emphasis of the program was on changing the environment, rather than addressing personality problems. The causal assumptions of the program were based largely on the opportunity theory of Cloward and Ohlin who helped design MFY. If opportunities for legitimate success were expanded, it was thought that delinquency would decline.

Unlike most programs that try to help juveniles adapt to reality, Mobilization for Youth tried to help people change reality. This goal was pursued by creating new employment opportunities, making juveniles more employable, providing students with tutorial help, providing day-care services, increasing the ability of local residents to influence the social and political life of their community, and many other activities.

Unfortunately, the effect of Mobilization for Youth on delinquency was only partially evaluated. Between 1962 and 1966 juvenile arrests were down somewhat in the MFY area, but they were up slightly in surrounding areas. In addition to the use of official statistics, which may reflect police practices more than delinquency, there was also a high tenant turnover in this area. Several low-income housing projects were also built during this period, so it is likely the number of juveniles in the neighborhood increased overall. These factors serve to confound any clear-cut effect of the program.

There are probably a number of reasons why Mobilization for Youth was unsuccessful. It is possible, for instance, that the theory upon which it was based was not comprehensive and could not be expected to account for the delinquency of an entire neighborhood.

One of the difficulties with the theory was that it could not and did not explain all delinquency, and was thus not "comprehensive" in that sense. There is more to delinquency than absence of opportunity, even among juveniles who suffer from that absence. It followed therefore that the program built upon the theory could not be truly comprehensive [Finckenauer, 1982].

Moreover, it may have been overly optimistic to expect to change an entire neighborhood in just a few years. Social change may be more complex and unwieldy than the founders of MFY realized [Weissman, 1969].

CLASSICAL v. POSITIVE APPROACHES TO PREVENTION

As discussed in Chapter 3, there are two schools of thought in criminology concerning the reasons why people behave as they do: classical and positive. According to the classical school, human behavior is the product of free-will. The positive school holds that behavior is the product of internal or external influences.

The vast majority of attempts to explain delinquency are based on positivism and, therefore, most prevention programs are based on positivistic assumptions. Both the Cambridge-Somerville Youth Study and Mobilization for Youth were based on the assumptions that psychological or sociological influences was the cause of delinquency. Clearly, if the causes of crime are seen as biological, psychological, or social, a successful crime prevention strategy is going to have to correct these influences, or else correct the juvenile's response to them. This is the fundamental assumption behind rehabilitation. That is, something needs correction and the prevention program aims to do this through rehabilitation.

The classical school, on the other hand, sees the exercise of free-will being guided by an individual's attempt to maximize pleasure and minimize pain. According to this view, the reason why everyone is not a criminal is due to the penalties for law violation. This is known as deterrence, which means that the threat of punishment will keep people from committing crimes by the example of those who are caught. Incapacitation or retribution as purposes of punishment are more applicable to secondary prevention in that they are designed as responses to law violation, rather than primary prevention which deterrence hopes to achieve.

If you believed that juveniles committed crimes not because of internal or external influences but, rather, that delinquency was a product a free-will, your prevention approach would be one that attempted to maximize pain and minimize the pleasure of delinquent acts. Furthermore, if you wished to achieve this, several conditions would have to be met--all of which are important to the notion of deterrence. For example, when you were a child and your parents said, "Do not touch the cookies or you will be sent to bed without dinner," what actually kept you from touching the cookies? Was it because your parents were actually going to send you to bed, or was it because you believed you would be sent to bed? Clearly, the actual chances of being caught are not as important as what you believe the chances are. As a result, deterrence depends more on perceived risk than it does on actual risk.

Although there is often a relationship between perceived risk and actual risk, it is surprising how weak the relationship often is. Studies of the fear of crime have shown, for example, that there is often very little relationship between people's fear of being mugged and their actual chances of being mugged [McIntyre, 1967]. Likewise, a study of high school girls found their expectation of being arrested was much higher than the actual probability of being arrested [Handler and Vitoux, 1978]. Therefore, what we believe to be true affects our behavior much more than the actual truth.

Other factors must also operate if juveniles are to be deterred from delinquency. First, it has been found that the severity of the penalty is of little importance in crime prevention [Silberman, 1980]. This is because the penalty must only outweigh the pleasure of the act. In fact, in some cases, extremely severe punishments have had the opposite effect and have increased recidivism, rather than reduced it [Eysenck, 1970]. This may be because very severe punishments negate any perceived relationship between the offense and the punishment, or such severity may even legitimize the use of aggression in the eyes of the recipient.

In addition to the importance of perceived risk, the certainty of the penalty is also very important to deterrence. If you are planning to commit a burglary, and realize the chances of being caught are small, it is unlikely you will be deterred, regardless of the possible penalty for the offense. Even if the penalty is doubled or tripled, it will make no difference to the offender because the odds of being caught are unchanged. This is because the possibility of being penalized is not considered by the offender. As Finckenauer has pointed out,

> ...we may all be gamblers at heart. We are interested in knowing what the odds are, and in our chances of beating these odds. Kids know that the odds on their beating the law are pretty good.

The swiftness between the act and penalty is also important to deterrence because it helps to connect the illegitimate pleasure to the pain of the penalty. A final aspect of deterrence that is very important to prevention is rationality. Deterrence assumes that people consider the consequences of their actions. That is, if you never think about getting caught, you will never be deterred from committing a crime. Therefore, spontaneous acts, acts committed under the influence of alcohol or drugs, and acts committed under emotional duress, are not deterrable.

Equipped with an understanding of the factors necessary to make deterrence work (namely, high perceived risk, certainty and swiftness of punishment, and rationality in commission of crimes), it is appropriate to examine the extent of empirical support for the idea of deterrence. In 1967, Daniel Claster examined the deterrent effect of the perceived risk of being arrested and convicted. He compared the risk perceptions of two groups of boys: one group was incarcerated for committing a delinquent act, while the other group was boys with no official record of delinquency. Claster looked at the accuracy of their perceived risk of being caught and convicted for certain crimes and the likelihood that they might commit delinquent acts in the future. Interestingly, he found no significant difference in the knowledge of the risks betweens the two groups, but he found that incarcerated boys were more likely to think they could get away with committing new crimes in the future. Ironically, these findings suggest that incarceration may <u>increase</u> the likelihood of criminality rather than deter it.

In 1978, Lotz, Regoli, and Raymond repeated Claster's study and found the same result: incarceration had little or no deterrent effect on juveniles. Looking back to the factors necessary for deterrence to work, it is possible that delinquency does not meet the assumptions implicit in deterrence. For instance, juveniles may not consider the consequences of being caught, or being caught and punished may reduce the fear of it happening again. Further, juveniles may commit crimes for reasons other than a free-will choice to maximize pleasure, while minimizing pain.

Other investigations that have examined the deterrent effect of criminal sanctions have found similar results. A review of a number of these investigations concluded, "there is not yet any clear or cohesive support for deterrence" [Anderson, 1978].

Similar to positivistic approaches to delinquency prevention, which are often based on psychological or sociological treatment, classical approaches also can take different forms. One major type of delinquency prevention strategy that employs classical assumptions is behavior modification. Behavior modification is conditioning, based on learning, where behavior is encoruaged or discouraged through the use of rewards or punishments. Rewards (or positive reinforcement) have been used very often to promote conforming behavior. Several juvenile institutions have been run on token economies where juveniles receive tokens for conforming behavior, which can be exchanged for merchandise or for special privileges. Some undesirable side effects of positive reinforcement are that it may produce manipulative behavior, rather than conforming behavior. Also, once outside the program, positive reinforcers will not follow conforming behavior, so the effect wears off quickly [Albanese, 1984; Sage, 1974].

Another type of delinquency prevention program based on classical assumptions is aversive techniques. Aversive techniques are actually a type of behavior modification which is based on negative reinforcers (or punishment). Fines, electric shock, and corporal punishment are examples of negative reinforcers.

A 1977 review of behavior modification studies was conducted of work published between 1968 and 1976. Of the 27 studies reviewed, only one dealt with delinquency prevention. The authors concluded that there was "a failure to show the relationship between successful behavior change and a subsequent reduction in measures of delinquency" [Emery and Marholin, 1977]. A 1978 review of the literature by Ross and McKay had a similar result. Despite the apparent lack of success of behavior modification programs in the prevention of delinquency, however, interest in these methods continues.

THE LIFER'S PROGRAM: SCARED STRAIGHT?

The attempt at delinquency prevention portrayed in the documentary film, "Scared Straight," has sparked new interest in the use of behavior modification techniques. The program is not based on positivistic assumptions because it does not assume that delinquency is caused by internal or external influences. Rather, it is based on the classical assumption that all juveniles are equally capable of committing delinquent acts, and that the program attempts to guide the exercise of free-will by deterrence. That is to say, once juveniles are aware of the possible consequences of their actions, this program (called the "Juvenile Awareness" or "Lifer's" program) hopes that juveniles will be prevented from committing future delinquent acts.

Several variations of this program exist in a number of prisons around the country. The format, however, is generally the same. A group of juveniles (normally, those who have had some previous contact with police) are brought to a prison where they are lectured, confronted, or even scolded for several hours by long-term inmates who attempt to demonstrate through their descriptions of prison life and their own attitudes as youngsters, how delinquency can lead to serious consequences.

Several of these programs have now been evaluated, which enables us to assess their effectiveness in preventing delinquency. James Finckenauer compared two matched groups of juveniles, one of which participated in the Lifer's program and the other group which did not. He followed each group for six months after their visit to Rahway State Prison in New Jersey (where the documentary film was made). His results are summarized in Table 2.

As Table 2 indicates, the experimental group (who participated in the program) did significantly worse after six months than did the control group. Those juveniles who did not go to the Lifer's program were significantly less likely to commit crime ("fail") than were those who participated.

Table 2. Delinquency Involvement Six Months
         After Lifer's Program Participation.

	Success	Failure	Total
Experimentals	59%	41%	57%
Controls	87%	11%	43%
Total Juveniles	58	23	81

Source: Finckenauer, 1982.

Finckenauer also examined the average seriousness of the subsequent offenses committed by both the experimentals and controls to see if there were differences in the types of offenses committed by the two groups. His results were the same.

> The results... reinforced the earlier finding that the experimental group did significantly worse than the control group in terms of outcomes. More experimentals than controls committed subsequent offenses and their mean seriousness of subsequent delinquency scores was significantly higher. As a subsample, the non-delinquent experimentals did worse than their nondelinquent counterparts in the control group [1982:138].

Finckenauer next controlled for age, sex, race, prior record, and predictive risk category to see if any of these additional factors accounted for his results.

> ...once the effects of all other variables...have been accounted for, the experimental-control group factor is still significantly correlated with subsequent offenses. This means that any differences in the characteristics of the two groups are not causing the differences in outcomes between them. It simply reiterates the conclusion that those juveniles who visited Rahway and confronted the Lifers behaved considerably worse after their visit than did the juveniles who did not visit [1982:140].

Therefore, the Juvenile Awareness Program appears, at best, to have no effect on delinquency and, at worst, makes its participants worse than those not attending.

Similar programs conducted in other states have had similar results. The JOLT (Juvenile Offenders Learn Truth) program at a Michigan prison was evaluated by the Michigan Department of Corrections in 1979. After following 227 experimentals and controls for three to six months, they found, "no measurable benefit for those juveniles who toured the prison" [Yarborough, 1979]. An evaluation of another program at San Quentin prison also found it to have no effect on delinquency.

> It was clear that the San Quentin Squires Program did not prevent subsequent delinquency among previously very delinquent youth. Overall, no statistically significant differences were found between experimentals and controls at 12 month behavioral follow-up.

The conclusion to this evaluation provides an indication of why these programs have not been successful.

> From a review of the literature on deterrence theory and juvenile awareness programs and the findings in this evaluation, our conclusion is that serious delinquency cannot be turned around by short-term programs such as Squire, Rahway, JOLT, etc. [Lewis, 1981].

As indicated earlier, prevention programs based on classical notions of delinquency have not generally been successful. Because juvenile awareness programs do not address the factors important to deterrence, it should not be surprising they are unsuccessful. Clearly, they cannot affect the certainty or swiftness of being caught, nor can they affect the rationality of juvenile conduct. Therefore, the inability of these programs to deter delinquency is a logical result.

WHAT WORKS?

Fortunately, delinquency prevention has had some success stories as well. Some types of programs have even been shown generally to be successful. Nevertheless, many efforts continue to be unsuccessful. The reasons for their success or failure is the most important concern, however, because knowledge of their strengths and shortcomings may help to avoid unsuccessful efforts in the future.

If you recall, the assumptions of Shaw and McKay and Walter Miller are quite similar. Both their theories assume that delinquency is the result of attitudes or values either caused or reinforced by peers, the environment, or by lower-class culture in general. A delinquency prevention program based on these assumptions would probably attempt to expose juveniles to the standards and values of the dominant culture and move them in that direction.

An example of a delinquency prevention program based on these assumptions is street-corner workers. Street-corner workers make contact with juvenile gangs, gain their acceptance, and then attempt to direct their disruptive energies into positive channels. A review of six different street-corner projects, however, found that they were not only ineffective in reducing delinquency, but they also showed evidence of increasing the cohesiveness of gangs and, indirectly, increasing the likelihood of gang delinquency [Dixon and Wright, 1975]. As one evaluation reported,

> Gang workers in this project spent one-fifth of their time working with gang members... With 50 to 100 gang members in the neighborhood, and eight hours per week spent in contact with them, how much impact can reasonably be expected? It seems presumptuous to think that an average of five minutes per week per boy could somehow result in a reduction in delinquent behavior, even if it is matched by half again as much time with some of the significant adults around him [Klein, 1969].

As a result, street-corner workers do not appear to be an effective tool for delinquency prevention--either because of the reasons above, or due to the defects in the theory upon which the idea is based.

Labelling theorists, such as Becker and Lemert, believe that delinquency is promoted by the adjudication process, which stigmatizes juveniles in the public eye, or else may provoke a changed self-image of juveniles. Rather than looking at environmental factors, therefore, proponents of labelling theory look at the juvenile justice process itself.

An example of a primary prevention strategy based on labelling theory would be decriminalization. This would involve changes in the law to eliminate some behaviors that are currently subject to adjudication. Decriminalization of marijuana and status offenses are examples of recent efforts to reduce the jurisdiction of the juvenile court and, therefore, reduce the possibility that juveniles will be labelled delinquents or status offenders.

A secondary prevention program based on labelling is diversion, which includes alternatives to official processing in juvenile court. A review of eight juvenile diversion projects in California was conducted by Thomas Blomberg in 1979. He compared juveniles in diversion projects with a matched sample of juveniles who were officially processed by the juvenile justice system. He found the diversion clients to perform better in four of the projects (as measured by re-arrests), but worse in four others. Another review of juvenile diversion programs conducted by the California Youth Authority found three of 15 programs to be successful in reducing delinquency [Palmer and Lewis, 1980]. They found that for the successful projects, "no single approach would be recommended for all groups of youths." Also, the frequency of contact, informality, and personal concern for the youth characterized the three successful programs.

As you can see from this sampling, most delinquency prevention programs have not had much success in reducing delinquency. Perhaps the largest obstacle to progress in this field has been that relatively few prevention programs have been objectively evaluated. In 1967, Berleman and Steinburn reviewed the literature and found only five studies that used a comparison or control group. In 1975, another review by Dixon and Wright examined all delinquency prevention programs from 1965-1973. They came up with 95 projects that reported some kind of empirical data. Only one-half used some form of comparison group, and only 25 percent used randomized or matched subjects. Such comparison groups are extremely important in that they allow the investigator to know "what would have happened anyway?" without exposure to the particular program.

Based on their review of all the delinquency prevention projects they could find, Dixon and Wright concluded that recreation programs, individual and group counseling, social casework, and street-corner workers either show no effectiveness or are effective under very limited conditions. On the other hand, they found educational and vocational projects, community treatment programs, the use of volunteers and paraprofessionals, and youth service bureaus to show some signs of effectiveness in preventing delinquency.

In 1979, Gendreau and Ross conducted an even more recent review of 95 correctional treatment programs between 1973-1978. After examining the factors that characterized successful programs, they concluded that successful efforts relied on "a combination of several tools to treat criminal and delinquent behavior. The studies reviewed that relied on a single treatment method had notably less positive results."

If future attempts at delinquency prevention keep in mind that: (1) Prevention programs should be based on specific causes of delinquency, (2) People commit crimes for different reasons, so a single strategy will not work for everyone, and (3) The distinction between primary and secondary prevention is an important one; we will know much more about why juveniles misbehave than we do now. If prevention programs relied on these principles, rather than on a hit-or-miss formula, perhaps we would be closer today to truly effective strategies for delinquency prevention.

REFERENCES

Albanese, Jay S. Justice, Privacy, and Crime Control. Lanham, MD: University Press of America, 1984.

Anderson, Linda S. The Deterrent Effect of Criminal Sanctions: Reviewing the Evidence. Dallas, Texas: Paper presented at the Annual Meeting of the American Society of Criminology, 1978.

Berleman, W.C. and Steinburn, T.W. The Execution and Evaluation of a Delinquency Prevention Program. Social Problems, 14 [1967], 413-423.

Blomberg, Thomas G. Diversion from Juvenile Court: A Review of the Evidence. In F.L. Faust and P.J. Brantingham, Eds. Juvenile Justice Philosophy. St. Paul, Minn.: West Publishing, 1979.

Claster, Daniel. Comparison of Risk Perception Between Delinquents and Non-Delinquents. Journal of Criminal Law, Criminology, and Police Science, 58 [1967], 80-86.

Dixon, Michael C. and Wright, William. Juvenile Delinquency Prevention Programs. Nashville, Tenn.: Office of

Educational Services Peabody College, 1975.

Emery, Robert and Marholin, David. An Applied Behavior Analysis of Delinquency. American Psychologist, [October, 1977].

Eysenck, Hans J. Crime and Personality. London: Paladin, 1970.

Finckenauer, James O. Scared Straight and the Panacea Phenomenon. Englewood Cliffs, N.J.: Prentice-Hall, 1982.

Gendreau, Paul and Ross, Bob. Effective Correctional Treatment: Bibliography for Cynics. Crime & Delinquency, 25 [October, 1979], 463-489.

Handler, Ellen and Vitoux, Mary. The Overestimation of the Probability of Arrest: Support for Deterrence Theory? Dallas, Texas: Paper presented at the Annual Meeting of the American Society of Criminology, 1978.

Klein, M.W. Gang Cohesiveness, Delinquency, and a Street Work Program. Journal of Research in Crime & Delinquency, 6 [1969], 135-166.

Lewis, Roy V. The Squires of San Quentin: An Evaluation of a Juvenile Awareness Program. Sacramento: California Youth Authority, 1981.

Lotz, Roy, Regoli, Robert M., and Raymond, Phillip. Delinquency and Special Deterrence. Criminology, 15 [1978], 539-546.

McIntyre, Jennie. Public Attitudes Toward Crime and Law Enforcement. Annals, 374 [1967], 34-46.

Palmer, Ted B. and Lewis, Roy V. A Differential Approach to Juvenile Diversion. Journal of Research in Crime & Delinquency, 17 [1980], 209-229.

Powers, Edwin and Witmer, Helen. An Experiment in the Prevention of Delinquency: The Cambridge-Somerville Youth Study. New York Columbia University Press, 1951.

Ross, Robert and McKay, Brian. Behavioral Approaches to Treatment in Corrections: Requiem for a Panacea. Canadian Journal of Criminology, 20 [July, 1978].

Sage, Wayne. Crime and the Clockwork Lemon. Human Behavior, [September, 1974].

Silberman, Charles E. Criminal Violence, Criminal Justice. New York: Vintage, 1980.

Weissman, Harold H., Ed. Justice and the Law in the Mobilization for Youth Experience. New York: Association Press, 1969.

Yarborough, James C. Evaluation of JOLT as a Deterrence Program. Lansing, Mich.: Department of Corrections, 1979.

9. A VANISHING JUVENILE JUSTICE SYSTEM?

CURRENT TRENDS IN JUVENILE JUSTICE

It is interesting to note that despite the lack of evidence linking severity of penalty to deterrence, punishment is currently being emphasized more and more often in delinquency prevention programs. Furthermore, recent moves in juvenile justice policy suggest that the emphasis on due process is being replaced by a crime control orientation.

In 1973, the Institute for Judicial Administration of New York City and the American Bar Association (IJA/ABA) established a Joint Commission on Juvenile Justice Standards. Over 100 professionals drafted 23 volumes of standards which were completed in 1977. Although the IJA/ABA only has authority to recommend changes in law, their positions are often influential in the passage of new legislation. They recommended many changes in the juvenile justice system, which reflected shifting views toward the criminal responsiblity of juveniles.

The IJA/ABA standards reject the rehabilitative model and propose that juveniles be punished according to the se. iousness of the crime.

> The Joint Commission rejects prevailing juvenile correctional philosophy that follows the rehabilitative ideal. Instead, the Standards suggest a return to the sentencing principle of using coercive sanctions appropriate to the seriousness of the offense as a mechanism to punish. Moreover, legislatures should mandate specific dispositions and sentences rather than leave them to judicial discretion. Because of the repeated failure of previous rehabilitative efforts, the Standards set modest rehabilitative goals that are secondary in importance to punishment and to protection of public safety [Ketcham, 1977].

Such a recommendation clearly replaces any vestige left of the rehabilitative model with the crime control model, which assumes crime to be the product of free-will.

The Standards also recommend the establishment of a preliminary hearing for juveniles to determine probable cause before adjudication.

In accord with the rights of an adult criminal defendant, the Joint Commission recommends that a juvenile have the right to require the state to present evidence at a pre-adjudication hearing to establish the likelihood that a crime has been committed and that the juvenile is probably the one who committed it. This juvenile court proceeding is much like a traditional adult probable cause hearing... In fact, in most respects a juvenile's rights during the pre-adjudication stage should be identical to those accorded to adults unless the special protective aims of the juvenile justice system require otherwise [Ketcham, 1977].

As this proposal suggests, the procedures applicable to the juvenile justice system would become the same as those for adults. Other recommendations of the IJA/ABA include: the right to a trial by jury, the right to appeal, and mandatory transcripts of juvenile court proceedings.

It is clear from this limited sampling of the IJA/ABA standards that, if implemented, the juvenile and adult systems would be operating under the same procedures, the same hearings, the same sentencing rationale, and the same philosophy. Therefore, it appears that the trend away from the founding principles of the juvenile court is continuing. Furthermore, additional evidence also exists indicating a change in the fundmental philosophy of juvenile justice.

OUR NEWEST CRIMINALS

In September, 1978 the New York State legislature created a new category of criminal behavior aimed exclusively at juveniles. This new type of criminal is called a "Juvenile Offender." According to the New York State law, a "juvenile offender" is a 13-15 year-old who commits any one of the crimes summarized below.

A 13 year old who is criminally responsible for acts constituting murder [with intent to kill or by gross recklessness], and a person 14 or 15 years old who is criminally responsible for acts constituting murder [during the course of a felony, with intent to kill, or by gross recklessness]; a 13 to 15 year old found

criminally responsible for kidnapping for ransom
or to inflict injury, arson by fire or explosion
with a person inside the structure; assault using
a weapon or with intent to disfigure; manslaughter
with intent to assault or under extreme emotional
disturbance; forcible rape; forcible sodomy;
burglary with a weapon or causing injury; and
attempted murder and kidnapping.

The significance of this law lies in the fact that
juveniles found criminally responsible for these crimes can
now be sentenced as adults. Therefore, it is possible for
juveniles in New York State to receive prison sentences of
up to life imprisonment for these crimes.

During the first five years this law was in effect, there
were over 5,000 juveniles arrested for crime subject to
prosecution as adults. New York City accounted for more
than 85 percent of these arrests. From 1978 to 1982 there
were 830 convictions of juveniles for these crimes, most of
whom have been sentenced.

Six hundred and seventy-nine [679] of the 830
convicted juvenile offenders have been sentenced
as of [1982]. Two hundred and eighty [41%] of
those sentenced have received probationary terms
as youthful offenders and an additional 92 [14%]
have been sentenced to imprisonment for less than
four years as youthful offenders. Three hundred
and seven youths [45%] have been sentenced to
imprisonment as Juvenile Offenders. In total, 399
[59%] Juvenile Offenders have been sentenced to
serve time in Division for Youth facilities.
Seventeen youths [3%] convicted of second degree
murder have received sentences with maximum terms
of life imprisonment, 12 of whom were sentenced
during 1981 [New York State. 1982].

An incarceration rate of 59 percent for 13-15 year-old
juveniles provides a clear indication of a major change in
the outlook regarding the causes and prevention of
delinquency.

New York State has now sentenced 731 juveniles to jail or
prison as "Juvenile Offenders" since 1978. In addition, 61
percent of them were sentenced to terms of three years or
more and 27 have received life sentences. Although these
juveniles have committed serious crimes, it appears the

positivistic assumptions of the juvenile court have given way to the classical handling of juvenile crime according to the crime control model. This is further evidenced by the fact that 14 other states have now passed laws similar to that in New York State.

A CHANGING PHILOSOPHY IN THE SUPREME COURT?

The U.S. Supreme Court heard a case in 1984 that provides additional evidence of the changing views toward juvenile justice. The case involved a challenge to the New York State Family Court Act which authorizes the use of pretrial detention for certain juveniles that pose a "serious risk" of committing a crime prior to their court appearance. The facts of the case were summarized by the Court as follows:

> Appellee Gregory Martin was arrested on December 13, 1977, and charged with first-degree robbery, second-degree assault, and criminal possession of a weapon based on an incident in which he, with two others, allegedly hit a youth on the head with a loaded gun and stole his jacket and sneakers. Martin had possession of the gun when he was arrested. He was 14 years old at the time and, therefore, came within the jurisdiction of New York's Family Court. The incident occurred at 11:30 at night, and Martin lied to the police about where and with whom he lived. He was consequently detained overnight.
> A petition of delinquency was filed, and Martin made his "initial appearance" in Family Court on December 14th, accompanied by his grandmother. The Family Court judge, citing the possession of the loaded weapon, the false address given to the police, and the lateness of the hour, as evidencing a lack of supervision, ordered Martin detained under [New York's Family Court Act provisions]. A probable cause hearing was held five days later, on December 19th, and probable cause was found to exist for all the crimes charged. At the fact-finding hearing held December 27-29, Martin was found guilty on the robbery and criminal possession charges. He was adjudicated a delinquent and placed on two years' probation. He had been detained pursuant to [the Family Court Act], between the initial appearance and the completion of the fact-finding hearing, for a total of fifteen days.

This case of Schall v. Martin became a class-action suit involving a large number of juveniles who, like Gregory Martin, were detained for one to two weeks and then released or given non-incarcerative sentences. The legal questions posed by this case are two: (1) Does preventive detention under the New York State law serve a legitimate state objective?, and (2) Are the procedural safeguards in the law adequate to authorize detention of juveniles charged with certain crimes? The Supreme Court believed that answers to these questions were necessary to determine whether New York State's Family Court Act met the "fundamental fairness" standard required by the due process clause of the Fourteenth Amendment.

In answering the first question, the Supreme Court assessed the balance between the needs of the juvenile and the protection of the community.

> Preventive detention under the Family Court Act is purportedly designed to protect the child and society from the potential consequences of his criminal acts. When making any detention decision, the Family Court judge is specifically directed to consider the needs and best interests of the juveniles as well as the need for the protection of the community...
> The "legitimate and compelling state interest" in protecting the community from crime cannot be doubted... The juvenile's countervailing interest in freedom from institutional restraints, even for the brief time involved here, is undoubtedly substantial as well. But that interest must be qualified by the recognition that juveniles, unlike adults, are always in some form of custody.

The Court went on to claim that because children do not take care of themselves, they are subject to the control of their parents, and to the state (via parens patriae), if the parents do not adequately control the child. As a result, the juvenile's liberty may, "in appropriate circumstances," be subordinate to the state's parens patriae interest in controlling the child.

With regard to the adequacy of procedural safeguards to protect the juvenile, the Supreme Court believed they were satisfactory.

There is no indication in the statute itself that preventive detention is used or intended as a punishment. First of all, the detention is strictly limited in time [adjudication must take place within 17 days]...

We find no justification for the conclusion that, contrary to the express language of the statute and the judgment of the highest state court, [New York's detention provision] is a punitive rather than a regulatory measure. Preventive detention under the Family Court Act serves the legitimate state objective, held in common with every State in the country, of protecting both the juvenile and society from the hazards of pretrial crime...

In sum, notice, a hearing, and a statement of facts and reasons are given prior to any detention under [the Family Court Act]... Given the regulatory purpose for the detention and the procedural protections that precede its imposition, we conclude that [the preventive detention provision] of the New York Family Court Act is not invalid under the Due Process Clause of the Fourteenth Amendment.

The reasoning of the U.S. Supreme Court provides a clear indication of its support of the crime control model for juvenile justice. By placing the protection of the community above the needs of the child, the Court shows its preference for crime control and community protection over rehabilitation and treatment of the juvenile. The Court's holding in this case provides further evidence of the nationwide trend in making juvenile justice more like criminal justice.

Three justices dissented in this case, and they recognized the move toward treating juveniles as adults. The dissent attempted to show that neither the goals of due process or crime control are achieved through the preventive detention of juveniles.

The majority's arguments do not survive scrutiny. Its characterization of preventive detention as merely a transfer of custody from a parent or guardian to the State is difficult to take seriously. Surely there is a qualitative difference between imprisonment and the condition of being subject to the supervision and control of an adult who has one's best interests at heart. And the majority's depiction of the nature of confinement under [New York's law] is insupportable on this record. As noted above, the District Court found that secure detention entails incarceration in a facility closely resembling a jail and that pretrial detainees are sometimes mixed with juveniles who have been found to be delinquent. Evidence adduced at trial reinforces these findings...

Both of the courts below concluded that only occasionally and accidentally does pretrial detention of a juvenile under [New York's law] prevent the commission of a crime. Three subsidiary findings undergird this conclusion. First, Family Court judges are incapable of determining which of the juveniles who appear before them would commit offenses before their trials if left at large and which would not. In part, this incapacity derives from the limitations of current knowledge concerning the dynamics of human behavior. On the basis of evidence adduced at trial, supplemented by a thorough review of the secondary literature, the District Court found that "no diagnostic tools have as yet been devised which enable even the most highly trained criminologists to predict reliably which juveniles will engage in violent crime." The evidence supportive of this finding is overwhelming...

Second, [preventive detention] is not limited to classes of juveniles whose past conduct suggests that they are substantially more likely than average juveniles to misbehave in the immediate future. The provision authorizes the detention of persons without any prior contacts with the juvenile court. Even a finding that there is probable cause to believe a juvenile committed the offense with which he was charged is not a prerequisite to his detention.

Third, the courts below concluded that circumstances surrounding most of the cases in which [preventive detention] has been invoked strongly suggest that the detainee would not have committed a crime during the period before his trial if he had been released. In a significant proportion of the cases, the juvenile had been released after his arrest and had not committed any reported crimes while at large... Even more

-122-

telling is the fact that "the vast majority" of persons detained under [New York's law] are released either before or immediately after their trials. The inference is powerful that most detainees, when examined more carefully than at their initial appearances, are deemed insufficiently dangerous to warrant further incarceration.

The rarity with which invocation of [New York's law] results in detention of a juvenile who otherwise would have committed a crime fatally undercuts the two public purposes assigned to the statute by the State and the majority. The argument that [the law] serves "the State's 'parens patriae interest in preserving and promoting the welfare of the child,'" now appears particularly hollow. Most juveniles detained pursuant to the provision are not benefitted thereby, because they would not have committed crimes if left to their own devices... On the contrary, these juveniles suffer serious harms: deprivation of liberty, stigmatization as "delinquent" or "dangerous," as well as impairment of their ability to prepare their legal defenses...

The argument that [preventive detention] protects the welfare of the community fares little better. Certainly the public reaps no benefit from incarceration of the majority of the detainees who would not have committed any crimes had they been released.

The dissent attempts to show that the Court's decision in this case does little to protect the rights of juveniles and nothing to protect the community or the welfare of the juvenile charged with a crime. Because New York's preventive detention law is not supported by the due process or crime control models (under which the majority argued its holding), and because the law works against any rehabilitative purpose, the dissent argues that the law should be repealed.

Similar laws in other states have been challenged on these grounds as well, but this U.S. Supreme Court decision is expected to end the litigation [Mauro, 1984]. It becomes clear that, based on current trends in juvenile justice such as the IJA/ABA recommendations, new laws allowing juveniles to be tried and sentenced as adults, the growing use of preventive detention for juveniles, and trends in the police disposition of juveniles (discussed in Chapter 5), the juvenile justice system philosophy established in 1899 may well be vanishing.

REFERENCES

Ketcham, Orman W. National Standards for Juvenile Justice. Virginia Law Review, 63 [1977].

Mauro, Tony. Pretrial Jailing of Kids Upheld. USA Today, [June 5, 1984], 3A.

New York State Division of Criminal Justice Services. Semi-Annual Report of Juvenile Offenders in N.Y.S.. Albany, N.Y.: Division of Criminal Justice Services, 1982.

10. WHAT IS THE FUTURE FOR JUVENILE LAW VIOLATORS?

BEING REALISTIC ABOUT DELINQUENCY

If the best predictor of the future is the past, it is clear that the nature of juvenile justice has dramatically changed in recent years and that juveniles will be dealt with even more severely in the future.

Prior to the establishment of the juvenile court in 1899, juveniles were treated as adults in the eyes of the law. The rise of positivism and the rehabilitative ideal changed our outlook regarding the causes of human behavior, however, and resulted in the differential treatment of juveniles. The failure of the rehabilitative model to live up to its promise of scientific and humane treatment led next to concerns about due process during the 1960s through the mid-1970s. Beginning with changes in the juvenile court structure in California and New York, and continuing with the Supreme Court decisions in Kent, Gault, Winship, and Breed v. Jones, the constitutional protection of juveniles became an overriding concern during this period.

The late 1970s ushered in a third wave, however, leading us back toward the treatment of juveniles as adults. Recent trends in the police disposition of juveniles, the IJA/ABA standards, the growing popularity of Juvenile Offender laws, and the preventive detention of juveniles, are all manifestations of this renewed application of classical thinking toward juvenile misbehavior and the replacement of the rehabilitative ideal with punishment.

ACCOUNTING FOR TRENDS IN JUVENILE JUSTICE POLICY

These shifting views are somewhat difficult to understand, considering the trends in delinquent behavior. As we saw in Chapter 2, juveniles appear to be accounting for a smaller and smaller proportion of the crime problem. Juveniles now account for less than one-fifth of all police arrests and an even smaller proportion of the arrests for violent crimes. This trend has continued for at least eight years, and it shows no sign of abating.

Due to a decline in the birth rate, and an increase in life expectancy, the proportion of juveniles in the population will decline even further in the future. As Kingsley Davis has pointed out, 15-19 year-olds made up 10.5 percent of the United States population in 1890, while they comprise 9.8 percent today. By the year 2000, they will constitute only 7.8 percent of the population. As a result, it is somewhat difficult to understand society's increasingly punitive response to a rapidly diminishing problem.

Arnold and Virginia Binder attribute the increasing support for repressive treatment of juveniles to the media.

> The public needs to be exposed to reality, and not to sensational reports that feed mounting fears and anger. Dramatic headlines decrying the "senseless" beating of a child on the school grounds or the "unpredictable" assault on a police officer by a juvenile gang in broad daylight have a powerful effect on the public and are more than capable of overshadowing the undramatic truth--only one individual in 1,500 will be injured by a juvenile and only one in 120,000 will die at the hands of a youth [1982:3].

On the other hand, Emile Durkheim might have suggested that such a situation should have been anticipated. As certain crimes become less common (e.g., juvenile arrests), those that remain are often seen as being more serious than they were before.

> Imagine a society of saints, a perfect cloister of exemplary individuals. Crimes, properly so called, will there be unknown; but faults which appear venial to the layman will create there the same scandal that the ordinary offense does in ordinary consciousnesses. If, then, this society has the power to judge and punish, it will define these acts as criminal and will treat them as such... Formerly, acts of violence against persons were more frequent than they are today, because respect for individual dignity was less strong. As this has increased, these crimes have become more rare; and also, many acts of violating this sentiment have been introduced into the penal law which were not included there in primitive times [such as insults, slander, and fraud] [1895:68-9].

Regardless of the cause, however, the last 90 years has seen the process of juvenile justice undergo a complete a cyclical change: From the treatment of all juveniles as adults, to the invention of the juvenile court and the rehabilitative model, to the due process model, now to where we are almost back where we started. It is ironic, but in the 1980s, we are closer to treating juveniles as adults than at any time since the turn of the century.

REFERENCES

Binder, Arnold and Binder, Virginia. Juvenile Crime/Juvenile Justice: The Need for a Proper Perspective. The Justice Reporter, 2 [March-April, 1982].

Davis, Kingsley. Demographic Changes and the Future of Childhood. In L.T. Empey, Ed. The Future of Childhood and Juvenile Justice. Charlottesville: University of Virginia Press, 1979.

Durkheim, Emile. The Rules of the Sociological Method. [1895]. New York: The Free Press, 1964.

INDEX